BMI

v.

MINICOM

Eleventh Edition

Deposition File

Faculty Materials

BMI

V.

MINICOM

Eleventh Edition
Deposition File
Faculty Materials

Anthony J. Bocchino
Jack E. Feinberg Professor of Litigation, Emeritus
Temple University
Beasley School of Law

Donald H. Beskind
Duke University School of Law

NITA®
NATIONAL INSTITUTE FOR TRIAL ADVOCACY

Address inquiries to:

Reprint Permission
National Institute for Trial Advocacy
1685 38th Street, Suite 200
Boulder, CO 80301-2735
Phone: (800) 225-6482
Fax: (720) 890-7069
Email: permissions@nita.org

ISBN 978-1-60156-852-6
FBA1852
eISBN 978-1-60156-853-3
eFBA1853

Printed in the United States of America

Wolters Kluwer

Official co-publisher of NITA.
WKLegaledu.com/NITA

SUSTAINABLE FORESTRY INITIATIVE Certified Sourcing
www.sfiprogram.org
SFI-00756

Contents

Introduction

This is a contract action between Business Machines Inc. (BMI), the plaintiff, and Minicom Inc., the defendant. BMI claims that it entered into a contract to sell 100 gross of interlaced graphene computing platforms (known as ICP-73s) to Minicom for $500,000, plus shipping costs. BMI asserts that the parts were shipped to Minicom by National Parcel Service (NPS) and the shipment was lost while in NPS's possession. NPS is not a party to this litigation. Its liability is limited to $400.00 by their contract with the shipper. On this the parties agree. BMI asserts that once it delivered the goods to NPS, BMI had complied with its contractual obligations and the risk of loss transferred to Minicom. BMI claims that Minicom, by failing to pay for the parts, breached the contract and is seeking damages in the amount of $500,000, plus interest and shipping costs. Minicom defends by saying that the contract included a term requiring BMI to insure the shipment of ICP-73s. Minicom claims that the term was agreed to in one or some combination of the following ways:

1. Michael Lubell and Virginia Young, as agents of Minicom and BMI, respectively, entered into a verbal contract that required BMI to ship the goods insured for full value.
2. Michael Lubell and Virginia Young had a conversation in which Lubell told Young that he wanted to buy the goods and have them shipped fully insured. Ms. Young, acting within the scope of her authority by BMI, told him that was acceptable and to confirm his request on a BMI provided order form, and communicate the order by email or letter, which he accomplished by submitting an order form and also emailing a letter containing the terms of the agreement and although not on a BMI order form, the letter contained all the information required by the order form.
3. Michael Lubell sent a letter order by both email and BMI's order form. Both orders referenced the prior course of dealing between the parties (the only prior shipment in September of YR-2 that had been sent insured), and Lubell asked that the new transaction be handled per the same agreement.

Minicom has filed a counterclaim for past and future losses.

Minicom asserts that BMI's failure to insure the shipment of ICPs breached the contract and forced Minicom to purchase cover goods at a cost of $50,000 over the original contract price. Minicom also alleges that BMI's failure to deliver the ICPs cost Minicom a contract that would have resulted in a profit of $100,000. Minicom alleges that it also lost future profits.

BMI replied to Minicom's counterclaim by alleging that Minicom failed to mitigate its damages. BMI also denied Virginia Young was its agent for purposes of contracting with Lubell and Minicom.

Pretrial discovery has been completed. The applicable law is contained in the Pretrial Rulings and in the Proposed Jury Instructions.

All witness roles in this case file may be played by either a woman or a man. The facts should be altered to be consistent with the gender of the person playing the role of a witness (e.g., name changes).

All years in these materials are stated in the following form:

1. YR-0 indicates the actual year in which the case is being tried (i.e., the present year);
2. YR-1 indicates the next preceding year (please use the actual year);
3. YR-2 indicates the second preceding year (please use the actual year), etc.

Electronic exhibits can be found at the following website:

http://bit.ly/1P20Jea
Password: BMI11

Special Instructions

The following witnesses may be called by the parties:

Plaintiff: Christopher Kay

Virginia Young

Defendant: Elliot Milstein

Michael Lubell

A party need not call all witnesses listed as its witnesses. Any or all witnesses can be called by either party. However, if a witness is to be called by a party other than the one for whom he or she is listed, upon notice to opposing counsel, the party for whom the witness is listed (above) must provide and prepare the witness.

The calendar included in this file is the accurate calendar for the time periods shown.

~ YR-2 ~

September

Su	M	T	W	Th	F	Sa
1	2	3	4	5	6	7
8	9	10	11	12	13	14
15	16	17	18	19	20	21
22	23	24	25	26	27	28
29	30					

October

Su	M	T	W	Th	F	Sa
		1	2	3	4	5
6	7	8	9	10	11	12
13	14	15	16	17	18	19
20	21	22	23	24	25	26
27	28	29	30	31		

November

Su	M	T	W	Th	F	Sa
					1	2
3	4	5	6	7	8	9
10	11	12	13	14	15	16
17	18	19	20	21	22	23
24	25	26	27	28	29	30

December

Su	M	T	W	Th	F	Sa
1	2	3	4	5	6	7
8	9	10	11	12	13	14
15	16	17	18	19	20	21
22	23	24	25	26	27	28
29	30	31				

~ YR-1 ~

January

Su	M	T	W	Th	F	Sa
			1	2	3	4
5	6	7	8	9	10	11
12	13	14	15	16	17	18
19	20	21	22	23	24	25
26	27	28	29	30	31	

February

Su	M	T	W	Th	F	Sa
						1
2	3	4	5	6	7	8
9	10	11	12	13	14	15
16	17	18	19	20	21	22
23	24	25	26	27	28	

March

Su	M	T	W	Th	F	Sa
						1
2	3	4	5	6	7	8
9	10	11	12	13	14	15
16	17	18	19	20	21	22
23	24	25	26	27	28	29
30	31					

April

Su	M	T	W	Th	F	Sa
		1	2	3	4	5
6	7	8	9	10	11	12
13	14	15	16	17	18	19
20	21	22	23	24	25	26
27	28	29	30			

May

Su	M	T	W	Th	F	Sa
				1	2	3
4	5	6	7	8	9	10
11	12	13	14	15	16	17
18	19	20	21	22	23	24
25	26	27	28	29	30	31

June

Su	M	T	W	Th	F	Sa
1	2	3	4	5	6	7
8	9	10	11	12	13	14
15	16	17	18	19	20	21
22	23	24	25	26	27	28
29	30					

IN THE SUPERIOR COURT
IN AND FOR THE COUNTY OF DARROW
AND STATE OF NITA

BUSINESS MACHINES INCORPORATED,	)	
	)	
Plaintiff,	)	CIVIL ACTION
	)	YR-1:2342
v.	)	
	)	
MINICOM INCORPORATED,	)	COMPLAINT
	)	
Defendant.	)	

The plaintiff for its complaint against the defendant alleges:

1. At all relevant times, the defendant, Minicom Incorporated (hereinafter Minicom), was a Nita corporation authorized to do business within the State of Nita and having an office and principal place of business located at 724 Science Drive in Nita City, County of Darrow and State of Nita.

2. At all relevant times, Minicom was in the business of designing, manufacturing, selling, and distributing a device known as CyberShield.

3. At all relevant times, the plaintiff, Business Machines Incorporated (hereinafter BMI) was a Delaware corporation, maintaining a place of business at One Industrial Drive in Brookline, Massachusetts.

4. At all relevant times, BMI was in the business of manufacturing, selling, and distributing electronic office equipment, computers, software, and electronic and mechanical computer parts.

5. At all relevant times, Elliot Milstein and Michael Lubell were employees and agents of Minicom and held themselves out as such to BMI.

6. On or about January 6, YR-1, Michael Lubell sent an electronic order form and a letter attached to an email to BMI's Brookline, Massachusetts sales office ordering 100 gross of interlaced graphene computing platforms, which are electronic devices containing operating instructions for small computers. These parts are designated ICP-73 in BMI's catalog and price list. The terms of the sale were payment of the full purchase price of $500,000 within sixty days of delivery except that a credit of 2 percent was to be given for payment within thirty days of delivery and a service charge of 1.5 percent per month was to be added to any balance still outstanding sixty days after delivery.

7. Mr. Lubell utilized both an online order form and a letter attached to an email that made no special requirement for shipping, asking only the "usual agreement." Specifically, Minicom made no specific request for insurance. BMI fulfilled the order as requested and shipped via NPS without declaring excess valuation or purchasing a shipment insurance policy.

8. On or about January 17, YR-1, BMI delivered to National Parcel Service (hereinafter NPS) for shipment to Minicom a parcel containing one hundred gross of ICP-73s.

9. On or about January 27, YR-1, Minicom notified BMI that the shipment had not been received. BMI notified NPS and directed NPS to trace the missing parcels.

10. On or about February 14, YR-1, NPS informed BMI that the goods had been lost in transit. BMI received a check from NPS in the amount of $400.00, which represented NPS's maximum liability in the absence of declared excess valuation or insurance.

11. On or about February 14, YR-1, BMI notified Minicom that the shipment had been lost and forwarded NPS's check for $400.00, its limit of liability, to Minicom with the following endorsement: "Pay to the order of Minicom Incorporated." Minicom did not cash the check.

12. On or about March 3, YR-1, BMI sent a letter to Minicom demanding payment for the goods delivered to NPS for shipment to Minicom. As of the date of this action, no payment has been received.

WHEREFORE, the plaintiff prays for

1. $500,122.60 in compensatory damages;
2. interest as provided by the agreement between the parties; and
3. such other relief as the court deems just and proper.

JURY DEMAND

Plaintiff demands a trial by jury in this action.

NORRIS, KROLL & SIMON by:

Elizabeth Simon

Elizabeth Simon
One Hancock Place
Boston, Massachusetts 01771
(617) 872-9331
Attorney for Plaintiff
DATED: May 9, YR-1

RETURN ON SUMMONS

I hereby certify that on May 13, YR-1, the above complaint and the summons were personally served on Charles A. Horton III, attorney for Minicom Inc., in his office at Suite 400, First National Bank Building, Nita City, Nita.

James Bell

James Bell
Speedy Summons & Process Inc.

IN THE SUPERIOR COURT
IN AND FOR THE COUNTY OF DARROW
AND STATE OF NITA

BUSINESS MACHINES INCORPORATED,	)	
	)	
Plaintiff,	)	CIVIL ACTION
	)	YR-1:2342
v.	)	
	)	
MINICOM INCORPORATED,	)	ANSWER AND
	)	COUNTERCLAIM
Defendant.	)	

ANSWER

1. Paragraphs 1, 2, 3, 4, 5, 9, 11, and 12 are admitted.

2. As to Paragraph 6, it is admitted that Minicom ordered 100 gross of ICP-73s at a price of $500,000 by a letter sent via email and USPS. In all other respects Paragraph 6 is denied.

3. Paragraph 7 is denied.

4. As to Paragraph 8 and 10, the defendant has insufficient information or knowledge on which to form a belief and so leaves the plaintiff to its proof of the matters therein alleged.

COUNTERCLAIM

1. At all relevant times, Chris Kay and Virginia Young were employees and agents of Business Machines Inc. (hereinafter BMI) and held themselves out to Minicom Inc. (hereinafter Minicom) as such.

2. Before the transaction described in the plaintiff's complaint, on or about September 3, YR-2, Minicom purchased from BMI 100 gross of BMI's part number ICP-73, an electronic device used in personal cybersecurity devices. Under the terms of the agreement, as stated in an order contained in a letter sent to BMI from Minicom via email and USPS, BMI agreed to ship the goods via National Parcel Service (hereinafter NPS) and insure them for their full value. Minicom agreed to pay all shipping and insurance costs.

3. On or about September 6, YR-2, BMI delivered the shipment to NPS for delivery to Minicom. BMI declared excess valuation of $500,000 and prepaid shipping and insurance charges. On or about September 10, YR-2, the shipment was received by Minicom.

4. On or about September 23, YR-2, Minicom paid BMI $491,232.60, the total purchase price of the goods, less a 2 percent discount for prompt payment, plus shipping and insurance charges as provided in its agreement with BMI.

5. On or about January 6, YR-1, Michael Lubell, Vice President for Purchasing at Minicom, telephoned the office of Chris Kay at BMI's Brookline, Massachusetts, sales office. Virginia Young answered the phone. Michael Lubell told her that Minicom was placing an order for 100 gross of ICP-73s at the same price and under the same shipping and insurance terms as the September transaction. Virginia Young agreed to leave a message for Chris Kay conveying the substance of her conversation with Michael Lubell.

6. On or about January 6, YR-1, Michael Lubell sent by online order form and a letter attached to an email an order to Chris Kay at BMI's sales office in Brookline, Massachusetts, confirming the telephone conversation described in Paragraph 5 and stating again that the transaction was to be on the same terms as the September 3, YR-2, purchase described in Paragraph 2. The letter called on Chris Kay to notify Michael Lubell immediately if a sale on the same terms as the September transaction was not acceptable to BMI. No such notification was received.

7. BMI shipped the ordered ICP-h73s to Minicom via NPS without requesting or paying for additional insurance.

8. Minicom never received the goods it ordered from BMI on or about January 6, YR-1, because, on information and belief, NPS lost the shipment after receiving it from BMI.

9. On or about March 10, YR-1, after receiving notification from BMI that the shipment had been lost in transit and that BMI did not intend to send another replacement shipment unless the original shipment was paid for, Minicom ordered technically identical replacement ICPs from Exrox Incorporated. Those goods were delivered to Minicom on March 18, YR-1, at a cost of $550,000.

10. Between the date on which the shipment from BMI was due to be received, which was on or about January 27, YR-1, and the date on which substitute goods were delivered, which was March 18, YR-1, Minicom was unable to produce certain types of cybersecurity devices and, as a result, lost net profits of $100,000 and lost future profits yet to be determined.

WHEREFORE, the defendant prays for

1. $150,000 in compensatory damages;

2. past and future lost profits;

3. interest as provided by law; and

4. such other and further relief as is just and proper.

JURY DEMAND

Defendant demands a trial by jury in this action.

HORTON, STEIN & BENSON
Attorney for Defendant by:

Charles A. Horton

Charles A. Horton III
Suite 400
First National Bank Building
Nita City, Nita 80027 (720) 555-6464
DATED: June 2, YR-1

IN THE SUPERIOR COURT
IN AND FOR THE COUNTY OF DARROW
AND STATE OF NITA

BUSINESS MACHINES INCORPORATED,	)	
	)	
Plaintiff,	)	CIVIL ACTION
	)	YR-1:2342
v.	)	
	)	
MINICOM INCORPORATED,	)	REPLY TO
	)	COUNTERCLAIM
Defendant.	)	

1. Paragraph 1 is admitted as to Chris Kay. It is admitted as to Virginia Young, except as it relates to the making of contracts on BMI's behalf.
2. Paragraphs 2, 3, 4, 5, 7, 8, and 9 are admitted.
3. Paragraph 6 is admitted to the extent that BMI received the email with attached letter and the online order form from Minicom. All other allegations are denied.
4. As to Paragraphs 10 and 11, the plaintiff has insufficient information on which to form a belief as to the truth or falsity of said statements and therefore denies them.

AFFIRMATIVE DEFENSE

1. In failing to timely purchase replacement goods for those lost by NPS, Minicom failed to mitigate its damages.

NORRIS, KROLL & SIMON by:

Elizabeth Simon

Elizabeth Simon
One Hancock Place
Boston, Massachusetts 01771
(617) 872-9331
Attorney for Plaintiff
DATED: June 16, YR-1

IN THE SUPERIOR COURT
IN AND FOR THE COUNTY OF DARROW
AND STATE OF NITA

BUSINESS MACHINES INCORPORATED,	)	
	)	
Plaintiff,	)	CIVIL ACTION
	)	YR-1:2342
v.	)	
	)	
MINICOM INCORPORATED,	)	REQUEST FOR ADMISSION
	)	
Defendant.	)	

As permitted by the Rules of Civil Procedure, plaintiff requests that the defendant admit the following:

1. Within the business and trade of which Minicom and BMI are parties, it is the normal custom and practice of companies shipping goods to ship them prepaid, without insuring them or declaring excess valuation, unless specifically requested to do so by the buyer and agreed to by the seller or by some other person with an insurable interest in the goods.

NORRIS, KROLL & SIMON by:

Elizabeth Simon

Elizabeth Simon
One Hancock Place
Boston, Massachusetts 01771
(617) 872-9331
Attorney for Plaintiff
DATED: June 17, YR-1

IN THE SUPERIOR COURT
IN AND FOR THE COUNTY OF DARROW
AND STATE OF NITA

BUSINESS MACHINES INCORPORATED,	)	
	)	
Plaintiff,	)	CIVIL ACTION
	)	YR-1:2342
v.	)	
	)	
MINICOM INCORPORATED,	)	RESPONSE TO
	)	REQUEST FOR ADMISSION
Defendant.	)	

Defendant responding to plaintiff's first request for admission admits the matter asserted. By way of further response, however, a specific agreement between Minicom and BMI required BMI to declare excess valuation and purchase full value insurance against loss or damage to the contents of the shipment which is the subject matter of this litigation.

HORTON, STEIN & BENSON by:

Charles A. Horton

Charles A. Horton III
Suite 400
First National Bank Building
Nita City, Nita 80027 (720) 555-6464
Attorney for Defendant
DATED: June 30, YR-1

Materials Available to the Plaintiff

Statement of Christopher Kay[1]
July 22, YR-1

My name is Christopher Kay, but I go by "Chris." I live at 11 Darby Road in Brookline, Massachusetts. My wife, Andrea, and I have two children: Chris Jr., age eight, and Lisa, age five. Andrea has a master's degree from Yale and is a Certified Nurse Practitioner [CNP]. We have been married since YR-10.

I grew up in Westport, Connecticut, and went to the public schools. After graduating from high school in YR-18, I went to Williams College and graduated cum laude in YR-14 with a degree in economics. After Williams, I took a two-year financial analyst position with the World Venture Fund on Wall Street to meet the work requirement for business school. With that behind me and with Andrea supporting us by working as a nurse, in YR-11 I enrolled in the University of North Carolina's MBA program. I received my MBA magna cum laude in YR-9.

After business school, I took a job as a sales manager trainee with Business Machines Incorporated (BMI) in their Brookline, Massachusetts, office. I have been employed there ever since. BMI is an international electronics firm. We manufacture and sell supercomputers and electronic parts and equipment. My current job is sales manager for Subdivision II of the Eastern Region of BMI, in Brookline.

BMI divides its operations into five regions in the United States. Each region is divided into subdivisions. The Eastern Region has six subdivisions. My subdivision (II) is the largest in the Eastern Region. It is a sales fulfillment facility. No manufacturing occurs in Eastern Subdivision II. We employ 105 people at the Brookline facility. We have twenty-five warehouses on thirty acres.

As sales manager, I directly oversee the sales staff at the Brookline facility. That staff includes three assistant sales managers, six sales assistants, twelve deputy sales assistants, and a varying number of management trainees and support staff. I also oversee existing customer accounts, find new accounts, and sell products. My subdivision sells electronic parts used by other companies in manufacturing specialty computing products including mobile devices, computers, military equipment, and civilian and military products.

I have been promoted several times in my eight years with BMI. I went from management trainee to deputy sales assistant in YR-7, to sales assistant in YR-6, to assistant sales manager in YR-5, and to sales manager in YR-3, all in Eastern Subdivision II. Compared to others who began with me as a management trainee, my promotion rate has been the fastest in our subdivision. I plan to stay with BMI for my entire career. It is an excellent company with a bright future and great health and retirement benefits. My next promotion would be from

1. Witnesses should follow this statement as closely as possible, but testify spontaneously. If necessary, witnesses may make up information that they believe is consistent with the witness statement. If there is a material misstatement when compared to what is provided, defending counsel must take reparative action.

the subdivision level to the regional level. In fact, in January YR-1, I was being considered for promotion to sales manager for the Eastern Region, a position scheduled to open in June of that year due to a retirement.

That job would have been the first step to upper level management at BMI. It would have meant a substantial raise. My current salary is $160,000 per year; the salary range for a regional sales manager is $185,000 to $245,000, with the possibility of bonuses ranging up to $30,000 per year. I could have also expected salary raises from wherever I started based on performance.

I did not get that promotion. I can't say for sure why I was passed over, but this problem with Minicom may have contributed. The woman hired, however, had been with BMI for five more years than I and was well qualified. I am sure I will be considered for other promotions, especially after this matter gets cleared up.

When we first did business with Minicom, I had been in my present position for about a year. Virginia Young has been my administrative assistant since YR-7, when I became a deputy sales assistant. While I was a management trainee, Virginia did some work for me out of the assignment pool. We got along well, so when I was eligible for my own administrative assistant, I asked her to work for me full time, which was a promotion for her. We have been a good team ever since. Each time I was promoted, I asked her to come along as my administrative assistant. I intended to bring her to the regional position if it had been offered. I don't know whether she would have accepted. It never came to that.

Virginia is married to one of my assistant sales managers, Casey Macon. They started dating after my wife introduced them at a holiday party at my house in YR-4 and married the next year. Virginia handles most of the purely administrative duties associated with my position. She takes care of most of my correspondence, maintaining my filing, taking phone messages when I am out, and making and tracking my appointments. She takes phone messages because it is company policy for sales offices not to use voice mail—we want customers to talk to a real person every time they call. BMI is paperless. Everything we receive on paper is scanned into our digital files, as are copies of paper documents we send out to others but want kept.

Virginia is well versed in the operation of our office. She routinely processes orders, and she is authorized, when I am not available, to electronically sign routine correspondence, like form thank-you letters for orders. Virginia often has direct customer contact. Customers tell me they appreciate how efficient she is and how well she treats them. She answers my phone when I am out or busy, answers emails for me, and often informs customers about product pricing and availability. She is not, however, authorized to enter into contracts on behalf of BMI. In my subdivision, contracts may be authorized only by me or one of my assistant sales managers.

In YR-2, a growing market for us was the cybersecurity industry. These companies make products protecting everything from mobile phones to the military. I first learned about

Minicom in July of that year, having read about the company in several trade journals. Much of what I am telling you today was refreshed when I reviewed BMI's digital file of everything relating to Minicom as a client. This file is kept on our server. I produced a copy of that electronic file and other electronically stored information that our lawyers provided to you.

I first heard of Minicom when I ran one of my periodic Internet searches to learn about new companies that might be potential BMI customers. Minicom popped up as a new player in the civilian cybersecurity market and therefore a potential customer for our electronic parts, especially our interlaced graphene computing platform [ICP]. These platforms use graphene, an extremely light and efficient material. Graphene chips create exponentially more addressable, programmable computing power on much smaller platforms. I researched Minicom in the "trades" and learned that they planned to enter the personal cybersecurity market with add-on products to iPhone and Android phones as well as tablet devices. Before the introduction of graphene chips, such products would be too heavy, large, and cumbersome for personal cyberspace security use. The word was that Minicom had a leg up on the technology for this potentially huge market. I believed BMI could forge a profitable relationship with them.

Right around the first of July of YR-2, we emailed them a with a link to the webpage for our ICPs. Exhibit 1 is a copy of the email sent to Minicom. As you can see, the email has a link to the ICP webpage and an "order" link directly to our digital order form. We switched to an online ordering system a few years ago and it works well so we encourage all customers to order online. Online ordering has virtually eliminated errors as the form provides for all necessary information. Over 80 percent of our clients order online, but since we still have customers who resist ordering on the Internet, we do take written orders by mail (including private providers like UPS) or written orders attached to an email. Requiring a writing limits the possibility of misunderstanding what our clients want and ensures a smoother delivery system. Exhibit 1A is a printout of the pricelist I sent to Minicom, and Exhibit 1B is a printout of our electronic order form.

The first time I spoke to anyone from Minicom was in early September of YR-2. Michael Lubell called me and said he was the vice president for purchasing at Minicom. He told me he was surveying ICP manufacturers. He had a copy of our ICP price list and was interested in purchasing 100 gross of ICPs. We discussed the technical requirements for the ICP they designed into their CyberShield product and identified the ICP-73 as the platform that suited their needs. Lubell seemed well versed in the technical end of his needs, so the identification process was simple. He did not, however, seem as fluent in the business end of the transaction.

In that phone call, I confirmed our price was $5,000 per gross. Mr. Lubell said he would like to place the order with me. I explained BMI's policy not to accept phone orders, because written orders prevent errors. I asked him to order online using the "order" button on the webpage, or send a written order in another form. I told him the online order form would be forwarded directly to my office. I said that written orders could be attached to an email or sent via USPS. Despite that discussion, he still asked to place his order over the phone. I again explained our policy, the reasons for it, and the need for a written order.

It is true that we will take a phone order in rare circumstances. Because Minicom was a new customer, I did not tell Mr. Lubell about that exception as it would not apply to him. In emergency circumstances, however, for long-term customers only, we will take a phone order. I am the only person in my subdivision authorized to make the exception to BMI's no phone orders policy, and I have done so only twice since I became sales manager for this subdivision. In both cases, the customer had been with us for over five years and averaged seven to ten orders per year. Our business relationship with them was well settled, and even in those circumstances we asked the customer to memorialize the order in writing before the order left the warehouse. The ability to take a "phone order" allowed us to begin processing the order without waiting for the written order.

In that first conversation, Lubell told me he needed the order shipped in ten days. I said National Parcel Service (NPS) was our preferred shipper, which was acceptable to him. I confirmed our payment conditions as they appear in our order form: a 2 percent discount for payment within thirty days; billing price for payment within sixty days; and 1.5 percent finance charge for each thirty-day period, or part thereof, for payments after sixty days of billing.

Lubell wanted us to declare excess valuation or otherwise insure the shipment to protect Minicom if the shipment was lost or damaged after it left our hands. Excess valuation means we tell the shipper the goods are worth more than the $400 per carton coverage the shipper automatically provides for free on all shipments.

The industry standard for shipped orders is that responsibility for the shipment shifts to the buyer as soon as the product is placed in the control of the shipper by the seller. In other words, BMI's responsibility for any shipment ends as soon as the shipper picks up the boxes. Because of that, purchasers are responsible if anything goes wrong—they still have to pay for the product, even if it's lost or damaged. This is why they need insurance.

Lubell's insurance request was unusual for our industry—most companies have "blanket" risk-of-loss policies that cover all incoming shipments—but when we received his written order we followed his directions and obtained the coverage. After our first conversation, Lubell eventually put all these terms of the order in letter form (he did not use an order form). We received the letter by both USPS and as an email attachment, although either of them would have been sufficient. Exhibit 3A is the email, 3B is the email attachment, and 3C is the letter. We received the email the day of our conversation, and the letter several days later.

When Ginny opened the email with letter attachment, she showed it to me because Minicom was a new customer. Otherwise, I do not usually review orders unless there is some question about the order. Ginny handles routine orders. I had Ginny process Minicom's order. She sent a work order to the warehouse that stocks ICPs (Exhibit 4). The order was shipped with a declaration of excess valuation via NPS (Exhibit 6). Once shipment was made, Virginia sent Minicom an email (Exhibit 5A) with a form thank-you note from me for their first order (Exhibit 5B), and an invoice (Exhibit 5C) attached to the email. The purpose of the letter and invoice is two-fold: to say thanks, and to be sure we have shipped out the right goods on the right terms. I hoped Minicom would become a long-term customer for us. I also reminded Mr. Lubell of the convenience of our online order form for future business. At any rate, apparently the parts were in good order, because we received payment within thirty days. Per our policy, Minicom got the 2 percent discount on the order (see Exhibits 7A and 7B).

Hoping to nurture our business relationship with Minicom, I invited a representative to our Eastern Regional Products Exposition in Hilton Head, South Carolina, in December of YR-2. Each subdivision sales manager can wine and dine potential and long-time customers. I invited thirty of my customers to this event. Little or no business is transacted during Expo, but good business relationships are fostered, which often lead to new or increased sales. After checking around, I determined that Minicom was a small company that was the brainchild of its president and CEO, Elliot Milstein. I invited him instead of Lubell, whose position at Minicom was the rough equivalent of a mid-level buyer at BMI.

I spoke with Mr. Milstein in November of YR-2, and he said he was interested in attending, especially after I told him we would pay all expenses for both him and his spouse, including hotel, meals, golf, and airfare. I confirmed his attendance by email, which was sent with a formal invitation (see Exhibits 9A and 9B).

During Expo at Hilton Head, I had several conversations with Milstein. He was bright, friendly, and easy to get along with, although he knew little about the business and purchasing aspects of the electronics industry. That made sense when he self-identified himself as a "techno-geek" with a PhD from MIT. He had worked primarily in research and development at NotYours, Inc.—a now defunct intra-office privacy/security company—so he was new to the sales, purchasing, and manufacturing end of the industry.

After playing a round of golf with Milstein, I talked to him specifically about purchasing parts for his business. He was particularly interested in our graphene ICPs, which he had ordered and used successfully. I told him that a coming increase in graphene prices was virtually certain to cause an industry-wide, 10 percent price hike in the cost of ICPs on March 1, YR-1; if he thought he would need another shipment of ICPs, he should order them before then. He said he anticipated needing another shipment to fill an order from a major retailer. The CyberShields were to be delivered in early spring YR-1 to their purchaser.

We also talked about Minicom's September YR-2 order with shipment insurance. I told him that the industry standard was for companies to purchase a "blanket" risk-of-loss policy rather than buying insurance for each individual shipment. A blanket policy covers all a company's incoming shipments for a lot less money than individual shipment insurance. He seemed surprised to hear about such a thing and said he would look into getting a policy when he returned home. Because a blanket policy is cheaper than what they were doing,

I was confident he would purchase such a policy. No, no one at Minicom ever told me they had gotten a blanket policy.

Those are the only two specific conversations about business I remember, although I'm sure we talked about the ICPs and other parts we sold that might be of use in his Cyber-Shields. By the end of Expo, I felt I had cemented our relationship with Minicom, and they would likely become a long-term customer. There were several other newer customers at Expo. They too appeared to be pleased with our products and service, and likely to become steady customers. Those new repeat accounts were important personally, because I was confident they would help me earn a favorable review for the Eastern Region sales manager, a position that, as I mentioned earlier, was coming open in the first half of YR-1.

The next time we heard from Minicom was in the first week of January YR-1. Virginia Young told me she had opened and responded to an email from Lubell (as I said earlier, Ginny opens my business emails and takes whatever action is required—usually providing information about product availability and/or price, handling a routine order, or telling me some action I need to perform like agreeing to contract terms). In his email, Lubell inquired about the availability of 100 gross of ICP-73s at the same price as their previous order. Exhibit 13 is a printout of that email, and Exhibit 14 is Ginny's response. As I said earlier, Virginia typically provides that information to customers; there was no need for me to be involved. I wouldn't even have looked at the email when it came in; that was Virginia's job. Yes, I see that the email (Exhibit 13) refers to shipping conditions, but that was unimportant as we will ship in any form that the customer requests, if they make their request clear in their order. This is especially so with a relatively new customer such as Minicom—for them and all customers, the order form or order letter controls the terms and conditions of an order.

On the day of the email, I was being interviewed off-site by the hiring panel from BMI's Eastern Region main office about the Regional Sales Manager position. After my last business meeting with them about the promotion I returned to the office, where I read an email from Ginny telling me that Lubell had called and wanted me to return the call (Exhibit 16). When I asked her to get him on the phone, she told me I didn't need to call him. She said that Lubell had wanted to talk about another order, but that she had told him to send an order form via the "order" button on the website price list or email. She said Lubell had since ordered using our order form, and also emailed an attached letter. Exhibit 17A is the email, Exhibit 17B is the attached letter, and Exhibit 17C is a printout of the electronic order form, also received by our office, ordering 100 gross ICP-73s. It was past normal business hours and I was scheduled for dinner with the interviewing panel, so I didn't see a need for me to return the call. I asked Ginny if there was anything unusual about the order, and she said it was standard, so I asked her to process the order. No, I do not believe I read Exhibits 17A, B, and C then, but it's possible I did. I reviewed them before meeting with you and the order did not call for anything special in terms of shipping or handling that I can see.

In processing the order, Virginia Young followed our normal procedure and sent a work order to the warehouse (Exhibit 18). She followed up with an email (Exhibit 19A) with an attached form thank-you note she signed on my behalf (Exhibit 19B) and an invoice (Exhibit 19C). That invoice clearly shows there was no insurance on the January YR-1 order.

Due to my conversation with Virginia Young, and the hectic atmosphere in the office surrounding my being interviewed for the promotion, I did not actually read the emailed order or the electronic order form until late February or early March, when this dispute arose. I know from the file that Ginny processed the order just as Lubell requested. Yes, Lubell claims he asked for insurance on the shipment, but as I had told Milstein, and as is stated on our order form, in our industry the custom is for companies to have blanket risk-of-loss policies. Without a specific request for insurance—like Lubell's request in September YR-2—a single shipment insurance policy is never purchased, because it would be redundant to the customer's blanket risk-of-loss policy.

Had I read Lubell's order on January 6, I would have interpreted it the same as Virginia Young did, and I would not have instructed her to purchase insurance for the shipment. Anyone at BMI or any other company in the industry would understand the language "per the usual agreement" to mean the usual agreement in the industry, which includes no excess coverage insurance.

In mid-January YR-1, we received a return of a shipment of ICP-22s that had been mistakenly sent to Minicom, together with a separate letter from Lubell (Exhibits 22A and B). It seems that order was sent out in error. Exhibit 21 is the NPS shipping record for that misorder. The letter billed us for shipping and insurance on that return and inquired about the shipment of ICP-73s. We paid for the return shipping and insurance right away. I emailed Lubell acknowledging receipt of his return and saying that in the unlikely event he ever had to return a shipment to us again, we had a blanket risk-of-loss policy so there was no need for him to insure returns. I also assured him that the ICP-73s had been shipped to him (see Exhibit 23). Yes, his letter did say something about us not billing them for insurance. I didn't really pay attention to that at the time.

When the shipment never got to Minicom, I called NPS. Exhibit 20 is NPS's shipping record for the ICP-73s for Minicom. Although they put a tracer on the shipment, they eventually had to admit that they had lost the parts. NPS sent us a check for $400, which was the limit of their liability, absent purchase of a shipment insurance policy. I mailed a letter to Lubell (Exhibit 26A) with the enclosed NPS check (Exhibit 26B) to Minicom. Again, we did not purchase insurance on the shipment because Lubell made no specific request for it. Based on my Expo conversation with Milstein, I believed Minicom would have had a blanket policy in effect by the January order. No, I had not received any such notice from Minicom. But I don't know why a company would not take the opportunity for substantial savings. Again, Lubell's instruction of "as per the usual agreement" on the order form did not indicate to Virginia Young that he wanted us to purchase insurance for the shipment, and even if I had reviewed the order I would never have interpreted that sentence to mean he wanted us to purchase insurance. I would read "usual agreement" as meaning the industry standard, and that standard is that responsibility for the product transfers to the purchaser upon shipment.

When I sent Lubell the NPS check in February YR-1, I told him we could fill another order of ICP-73s for Minicom and reminded him of the March 1, YR-1, price hike. As it turned out, Minicom did not have a blanket risk-of-loss policy in effect. When Lubell called about my letter, I explained to him that BMI bought no insurance on the shipment because he had not requested it. I also told him we had to bill him for the lost shipment. He seemed very upset, but there was nothing I could do about it. He did say that Minicom needed the parts to fill an order of CyberShields; I told him again that we could expedite another shipment to them.

Then Milstein called. He asked for me to see if there was any way we could replace the shipment, because he needed the platforms for an order he had to fill. I told him I would check it out with the legal department. I did not tell him it was unlikely we could replace the shipment because I hoped, despite the NPS screw-up, that we could keep Minicom as a customer. I forwarded his request to legal, and they clarified BMI's position: Minicom owed us for the lost shipment. They provided the letter that I sent to Milstein (Exhibit 30). The last I heard from Milstein was an angry letter he sent in March of YR-1, which I forwarded to legal. Eventually BMI sued Minicom, and now Minicom has sued us.

Statement of Virginia Young[2]
July 22, YR-1

My name is Virginia Young. I am twenty-nine years old and have been married to my spouse, Casey Macon, for three years. We live at 25 Scott Place in Brookline, Massachusetts. I work as Chris Kay's administrative assistant. Chris is sales manager for Eastern Subdivision II of BMI. Casey and I have no children yet. Casey works as an assistant sales manager under Mr. Kay at BMI.

I grew up in Nita City, Nita, and attended the public schools there. I am one of six children. My parents, all my siblings and their families, and many aunts, uncles, and cousins all still live in Nita City. My dad has been the head coach of the Nita University baseball team for the past twenty years. He is well known in Nita City. After graduating from Nita City High School, I attended Millbrook Community College in Conwell, Massachusetts, and graduated in YR-8 with a BS in sales and marketing. Unfortunately, when I graduated the job market was in a serious downturn, and I couldn't find a position that matched my qualifications, but I really wanted to stay in sales and marketing. My first position was in a temporary personnel pool that provided administrative and clerical services for people at the sales and distribution center in Brookline. I first met Chris Kay, who was a management trainee, while I was in the temp personnel pool. I did a project and some clerical work for him.

In YR-7, Chris was promoted to deputy sales assistant and was entitled to have a full-time administrative assistant; he asked me to work with him. We have been together ever since. My career has tracked his—every time he was promoted (from trainee to deputy sales assistant to sales assistant to assistant sales manager to sales manager) he asked me to continue to work with him. As his responsibilities increased, so did mine. And each promotion for him meant a promotion and a raise for me as well. BMI offers merit raises for employees recommended by their supervisors. Mr. Kay recommended me every year we've worked together. My current salary is $51,000 per year.

Chris has risen quickly within the ranks at BMI. He is considered to be on a fast track to senior management. He has moved up much more quickly than the other people hired at the same time as him as management trainees. In fact, two of his assistant sales managers have been with BMI longer than he, and several people from his management trainee year work under him as sales assistants.

Chris has been in his current job since YR-3, and in early YR-1 he was being considered for a promotion to sales manager for the entire Eastern Region. He told me that if he was offered the position, he wanted me to come along. That would have meant a raise for me to $64,000 per year. Because that would have meant a move to the regional office in Stamford,

2. Witnesses should follow this statement as closely as possible, but testify spontaneously. If necessary, witnesses may make up information that they believe is consistent with the witness statement. If there is a material misstatement when compared to what is provided, defending counsel must take reparative action.

Connecticut, he told me that he would try to find a good position for Casey in that office as well, adding that Casey was certainly qualified. We never had to cross that bridge, though, because Chris did not get that promotion. I am sure he will be promoted in the future, though—he is very good at his job, and a nice man to boot.

Chris is my only supervisor and handles my performance evaluations. My evaluations have always been excellent. For the past few years, he has had me fill in "excellent" (the highest rating) in all categories on the evaluation form and give it to him to sign and submit. Chris and I have a great working relationship. Chris calls me as his "right arm," and I work very hard to do a good job for him and BMI.

Chris and his wife, Andrea, have always taken good care of me. I have been a guest at his house for holiday parties and other company-related events. In fact, Andrea introduced me to Casey at a holiday party at the Kays' house. Naturally, I am very thankful for that introduction since we married a year later.

As Chris's administrative assistant, I handle his incoming and outgoing correspondence, screen his calls, open and respond to his emails, and process customer orders. I am authorized to prepare and sign form letters that go out over Chris's signature when Chris is unavailable, such as the form letter thank-you notes for orders into which I insert the particulars of the transaction. I frequently speak with customers over the phone or via email to provide information about the availability of products, price, and shipping and payment conditions.

I am not authorized to make contracts for BMI. Chris does that. BMI also has a strict policy that it does not take telephone orders. We are instructed to tell customers or potential customers that all orders must be made in writing. We encourage customers to use the online form, but we will accept orders made in emails or some other hard copy like USPS. We tell customers that our order form is available on our website and point them toward the link on our emailed price lists. We will of course provide the link over the phone, if requested. I know that Chris can waive the policy, but he's the only one in the office who can, and I don't remember him ever doing so. BMI's policy regarding orders has been in effect since I started with the company. We print it on all our price lists and brochures and it's on our website. Whenever I speak with a customer about a potential order, I always remind them that orders have to be made on our online order form or in some other written form.

Although there is no written policy on how I do my job (managers and administrative assistants work out how they will function together), Chris and I have developed a routine. For outgoing correspondence: Chris typically emails me with a rough outline of what he wants the letter to say; I draft and edit it, email it back; Chris makes any final changes and sends it back to me; I print out the final version for his signature, together with an addressed envelope. Sometimes he makes additional changes, but eventually I get a signed letter from him. Once that happens, I scan it to our digital files and add it to the customer's folder. That information can be accessed only by Chris or me. I also distribute any other copies shown on the letter or blind copies. As for the original, I fold it, place it in the envelope whose address matches the address on the letter, run it through the postage meter, and leave it for pick up by the mailroom people, who take mail to the post office twice a day. Alternatively, if speed is more important than the look of the correspondence, I attach a scanned letter to an email.

Our procedure for incoming correspondence, whether by email or standard mail, is as follows:

1. The mail is delivered twice a day at 9:00 a.m. and at 2:00 p.m. Email correspondence is received throughout the day on my computer—I have access to both my own email account and Chris's business account.

2. I open all mail and discard what is obviously junk mail. When in doubt, I keep the piece of mail. I stamp the correspondence as "received," with the date of receipt.

3. I scan all orders or other important correspondence to the customer's file after they are stamped as received, and then place all the mail on Chris's desk.

4. After he reviews the orders and mail, Chris tells me, either verbally or by placing a "post-it" on the correspondence, what to do with each piece of correspondence. Usually he has me do one or more of these things:

   a. confirm I have digitally filed it in the sender's folder;

   b. throw it away;

   c. complete a response he has dictate in the manner I described earlier;

   d. tell me to send a form response; or

   e. in the case of orders, tell me to process the order. This involves preparing a work order based on the written order and emailing it to the appropriate warehouse (different warehouses handle different products). The work order shows the name of the product and the amount of the product, the address of the customer, and any special shipping conditions such as ship by such-and-such date. I then prepare a thank-you note and statement of account to send to the customer.

5. For email, our process is similar:

   a. I open all Chris's emails and, again, delete what is obviously junk.

   b. I tag his emails: green for straightforward orders that he can review when he has time; yellow for orders that need his immediate attention; blue for business correspondence—such as customers who have deeper questions than I can answer, or emails from another BMI office; red for urgent matters; orange for anything personal.

c. After he reviews his email, if there is anything he needs me to do he will forward the email to me with instructions.

For simple requests such price lists, availability, and shipping times, I respond, using my email address, with the requested information and tag the email green. For simple online orders, the ones I label green, I process the orders in the same way I process orders that come by mail, though the thank-you note is by email and the statement is an attachment to that email.

The purpose of the thank-you note is to acknowledge the order and notify the client when the shipment was or will be sent and how. The statement serves as an invoice to be paid by the client. To be sure that we have correctly shipped the product in the amount and manner that the customer desired, the letter asks the customer to inform us if there are any errors in the letter or the statement of account. Our normal shipper is National Parcel Service (NPS).

No, I do not copy my responses to Chris; he trusts me to provide accurate information. If the email inquires about the availability of product for a potential order, I always remind the customer in my reply of BMI's policy that all orders have to be made either using the online order form or otherwise in writing.

The procedure for Chris's outgoing calls is as follows:

1. He will ask me to place a call to a particular person.

2. I will get the number either from our contacts list or an online phone directory and place the call, then:

   a. ask for the party;

   b. get the party on the phone;

   c. ask the party to hold for Mr. Kay; and

   d. notify Chris that his party is on the line, and then he takes the call.

3. As a result of the call, Chris may have me do a number of things, including:

   a. send a letter;

   b. retrieve some information and provide it to the customer, usually by email; or

   c. make a follow-up call.

For incoming calls:

1. I answer the phone saying, "BMI, Mr. Kay's office, Virginia Young speaking. May I help you?"

2. If the party asks for Mr. Kay, I'll get the caller's name and purpose for calling.

3. If the customer wants information that I have, I will provide it; but if the customer still wants to speak with Chris, I'll ask the party to hold to see if Mr. Kay is in.

   a. I notify Chris of the call and ask if he wants to take it; and either

   b. Chris will pick up the call; or if he is out or busy, I will take a message, which I send to Chris via email. Chris thinks voicemail is too impersonal, so I always take his messages.

If a customer tries to order one of our products over the phone, which is unusual, I always remind the customer that all orders must be made by mail (and provide the address) or on our online order form, offering to send a link to it if the customer so desires.

Orders that are sent using our online order form also come to Chris's email address. They are almost always straightforward and do not require Chris's attention. I review them and, unless there is a special request that needs Chris's attention, forward them to the warehouse.

I know that we had dealings with Minicom before the one that this lawsuit is about, but I needed to review all the materials that we found when I searched our server for the lawyers to refresh my memory about them. I am told BMI's lawyers gave you everything I found. From the file, I know that we emailed a price list for interlaced graphene computing platforms (ICPs) to Minicom in July YR-2 (Exhibit 1A) which, like all our brochures and price lists, has the link to the order form on our website. Minicom's first order was in September YR-2. I'm sure I answered the phone and connected the caller with Mr. Kay, because I always do. I do not remember speaking with anyone from Minicom in September, other than to answer the phone. I recognize Exhibits 3A and B as an email and order from Minicom. Yes, they emailed their order as a letter, even though I'm sure Chris followed our regular procedure and told them to use the online order form. Exhibit 3C is a USPS letter order from Minicom and a copy of the order letter; Exhibit 4 is the work order I prepared for that order. Yes, I did have that order insured because the order letter specifically requested us to do so. I was able to do so, even though they didn't use our order form, because the letter set out all necessary information. How Minicom ordered parts in September YR-2 was certainly not on my mind in January YR-1. We had processed over a hundred orders between the two from Minicom, and there was no reason for me to remember their September order in January of the following year. Exhibits 5B and 5C are the thank-you note and statement of account for the September order that I emailed; and Exhibit 7A is a letter I opened from Minicom containing their payment of our invoice (their check is Exhibit 7B). It was a routine order, other than being by an emailed letter. I only recall the details of that first order from reviewing the materials I collected from our server.

I do remember that Chris was happy about Minicom's new business with us because he decided to invite a Minicom representative to our Expo in Hilton Head, South Carolina, in December YR-2. Chris viewed Minicom as a potential long-term account. I handled all the correspondence for the Expo inviting Elliot Milstein and his spouse, including Exhibits 9A and 9B. No, I did not attend. I remained at the office and communicated several times a day with Chris about things that required his decision or input.

In January YR-1, I opened an email to Chris from a Mr. Lubell at Minicom inquiring about the availability of 100 gross of our ICP-73s. Exhibit 13 is a printout of that email. I responded to that email, saying the parts were available and confirmed the price and payment terms and asked that he place any order online by or mail. Exhibit 14 is a printout of my response. I have no reason to believe that the email exchange did not occur on January 3, YR-1, as shown on the email.

I don't know whether I said anything to Chris about the email. During the beginning of January, Chris was extremely busy preparing for a visit from head-office management, who were coming to Brookline to evaluate our facility and to interview Chris for the promotion to sales manager for the Eastern Region that I mentioned earlier. As a result, things were very hectic, and I doubt that I would have thought it important enough to show Chris such a routine email exchange.

A couple of days later, on January 6, YR-1, I answered a phone call from Mr. Lubell at Minicom. I remember the call because after I informed him that Chris was unavailable and asked if I could help him, he tried to place an order for parts over the phone. Although I do not recall what I said specifically, I am sure that I told him that his order had to be placed using our online order form or by mail, preferably on our order form. I offered to send to him a link, because that is what I always do. There is no chance that I took his order over the phone. I am not authorized to do so. That is something I would never do, and have never done.

I do not remember whether Mr. Lubell mentioned that he wanted to have his order insured, but I think if he had I would have remembered it because it would have been an extremely rare request. Most companies we deal with have a blanket insurance policy that covers all shipments we make to them, and my clear instruction from Chris, for as long as I have been processing orders for him at BMI, is not to insure a shipment and bill the customer for the insurance unless there is a specific written request from the customer for insurance. But no, I cannot swear that he did not mention insurance. That's because we go by the written order, so any terms he mentioned over the phone wouldn't have been important to me. As Chris explained many years ago, the customer can change his mind after the fact about orders, so we always go by the writing.

Mr. Lubell did ask for Chris to return his phone call, so I took the message and sent it to Chris as an email. Exhibit 16 is a copy of that email.

The day that Mr. Lubell called, we got an order from Minicom using our order form. Exhibit 17C is that order. He also sent a copy of the order as an attachment to an email Exhibit 17A is the email, and 17B is the letter version of the order. I don't know why he sent both an order form and an email—either one would have been sufficient. You are right that the email says that the letter is "confirming Minicom's phone order," but I do not attach any meaning to that language. The order form was the order, as well as the duplicate of it with the emailed letter, and since we had it, there was no reason to quarrel with Mr. Lubell's characterization that it confirmed anything. It certainly would not change the way the order was processed. Frankly, I don't know that I noticed the "confirming" language when the email came in. It was the order that was important. I do not remember whether Chris read the email order; probably not. I believe that, because he was so busy, I just told him that an order came in and that he told me to process the order, which I did.

Looking at the online order form and the emailed order, I would never interpret the order to be requesting insurance. I know that Minicom claims it does, but "the usual agreement" is, as I explained earlier, not to take out insurance unless it is specifically requested, and that request is simply not there. I handled this order just like I handle any other order to BMI—it was straightforward, and I labeled it green. Anyhow, if Mr. Lubell wanted insurance and failed to make a specific request, he should have called to tell us that there was an error in his statement of account provided with the thank-you note that asks the customer to do so if there is an error in the statement. Exhibits 19B and 19C are the thank-you note and the statement. If he had called and made it clear that he wanted insurance, I would have made sure he got it because their order didn't ship until after he got our emailed letter; it does not bill for insurance, because he didn't ask for it.

That was really the last I had to do with Minicom, other than referring calls to Mr. Kay, opening correspondence from them, and preparing correspondence to them. I do remember that Minicom sent us back a shipment of ICPs that was mistakenly sent to them by the warehouse. It is unusual for the warehouse to make such a mistake, but mistakes do happen from time to time.

Naturally, I had some conversations with Chris about the lost shipment back when it happened, but I did not say anything to him that I haven't told you. Those conversations were before this lawsuit started. Since then, we have not spoken about the case on the advice of our lawyer.

Materials Available to the Defendant

Statement of Michael Lubell[3]
August 17, YR-1

My name is Michael Lubell, and I live at 214 Burning Tree Drive in Nita City, Nita. I am thirty-one years old, and I am married to Dr. Ellen Scheps, who is on staff at Nita Memorial Hospital and on the faculty as an Assistant Professor at the Nita University Medical School. We have no children, but hope to start a family in the not too distant future. We met when I was a student at MIT and she was attending Harvard. Elliot Milstein was my roommate at the time, and his girlfriend (now wife) Zoe introduced her best friend Ellen to me.

Ellen and I actually grew up in the same part of Connecticut, although we never met before college. I graduated from Lyman Hall High School in Wallingford, and Ellen, whose family lived in neighboring Cheshire, went to prep school at Choate Rosemary Hall, which is located in Wallingford. We were married the summer after college graduation in YR-10, the same summer that Elliot and Zoe got married. We have been good friends with the Milsteins since our days in college.

As I said, Ellen is a medical doctor with a specialty in internal medicine. She earned her MD in YR-7 from Tufts University, and finished her residency and fellowship at Massachusetts General Hospital in YR-3. She is on staff at Nita University Medical Center and serves on the Medical School faculty as an Assistant Professor of Medicine.

After graduating from MIT with a degree in computer science, I enrolled in the MBA program at Boston University. I was accepted into the program without any previous business experience (which I was told by the school was unusual) only because of my expertise in the computer field, which the school viewed as a substitute for experience in the business community, at least with regard to information technology. The program was a two-year program. Even though I was in the top quarter of my class and in good academic standing, I left after one year, in YR-9. The program was geared for someone who wanted a career on Wall Street, and that wasn't me. I decided to apply to law school, so while I completed applications, I worked at an Apple Genius Bar in one of their retail outlets in Boston troubleshooting their products, apps, and software.

In YR-8, I started the JD program at Northeastern University School of Law in fall YR-8. I hated law school almost immediately, but stuck it out through the first year. I was doing fine academically. Northeastern does not have a traditional grading system, but I was in good standing. I left after exams in May YR-7 and decided to look for something else to do, but I could have gone back to Northeastern if I wanted to. For the next year, I worked as a paralegal in the patents department of the Smith, Liu & Roberts law firm in Boston. The pay

3. Witnesses should follow this statement as closely as possible, but testify spontaneously. If necessary, witnesses may make up information that they believe is consistent with the witness statement. If there is a material misstatement when compared to what is provided, defending counsel must take reparative action.

was good, and we needed the income to help pay for Ellen's medical school education, but I found the work tedious.

In the late spring of YR-6, a friend of mine from BU, John Staffier, approached me with a proposal to open up an electronics retail business specializing in high-end computer games, hardware, and games for Nintendo, Xbox, and PlayStation systems, and software geared toward the sophisticated student market. He had what he called a prime location in Cambridge, and by September YR-5, with loans from my parents and John's parents, we opened our store, called Techno-Toys. The shop was an instant success, and we paid off the parental loans with a line of credit provided by the bank. We did very well until a big box store opened up around the corner from us and essentially covered our market. With their volume sales pricing, they drove us out of business.

By January YR-4, we were out of business and into bankruptcy. While we were in the process of losing our business, I did something stupid. When our credit line ran out, I wrote some personal checks to try to restock our shop, and the checks bounced. I had hoped that sales would cover the checks, but that didn't work out. When I couldn't pay the checks (I was too proud to ask my parents or anyone else for help), I was arrested and charged with larceny. Because the amount involved was over $4,000, it was a felony with up to a two-year prison sentence.

My parents paid for a lawyer, who got me a deal. I pled guilty because I was guilty and got a one-year suspended sentence with two years' probation. As a condition of my probation, I had to pay a fine, court costs, and restitution. The restitution was to pay back all the checks with interest. I successfully completed my probation without any problems, and paid everything back with interest.

From February YR-4 until May YR-3, I worked as a salesclerk at a Verizon kiosk at the Galleria in Cambridge while Ellen was finishing her fellowship at Mass. General. We had agreed that when she completed her fellowship, we would move to wherever she received her best offer, so it didn't make much sense for me to try to find a career-type position. I tried to get my old job back at the law firm, but the conviction was a problem for them, so I just worked in retail sales for Verizon while I made enough to pay off the bad checks.

We ended up in Nita City for two reasons. First, Ellen got a great offer to go on staff and on faculty at Nita University's med school and Memorial Hospital. Second, Elliot Milstein offered me a position at Minicom.

We had remained very friendly with the Milsteins after graduating from college. For the first three years, Elliot was in a PhD program in electrical engineering at MIT. Zoe, who was an economics major, got her MBA from Harvard and worked for a year in an investment house in Boston. In YR-7, they moved to northern New Jersey, where Elliot worked for a computer security startup, NotYours, Inc. in research and design, while Zoe worked on Wall Street. In YR-4, NotYours was purchased by a Japanese conglomerate and Elliot cashed in his stock options, which I understand were worth quite a lot.

That was in late YR-4, and he and Zoe moved back to their hometown, Nita City. They planned to invest in opening a business, and wanted to start a family and be near their families in Nita City.

During the time we were all in Boston after graduation, we saw the Milsteins probably twice a month for dinner or a movie or something. After they moved to New Jersey, we talked on the phone or emailed regularly, and each summer we would get a place on the New Jersey shore for a week. Elliot is probably my best friend, and I think Ellen would say the same about Zoe.

In the early winter of YR-3, just as Ellen was trying to figure out which position she would take after her fellowship, I got a call from Elliot. He was going to start his own company, called Minicom. It was Elliot's idea to design and manufacture attachable hardware for phones and personal computers to protect the contents of the phones and personal computers from theft or manipulation. This was an idea he had been talking about for years, but NotYours was interested only in networked security systems.

Elliot had already designed the first product for Minicom in January, when we talked. Basically, it took advantage of newly available graphene interlaced chip platforms which could rapidly process all the information necessary to provide cybersecurity to consumers, who more and more kept valuable personal information on their phones and personal computers. He had tentatively called his product CyberShield, and he envisioned the first iteration of the product to be ready in late YR-3.

Elliot was very excited about the design's prospects. He had already obtained a lease on a warehouse on Science Drive in the Research Park in Nita City. The facility was being renovated, and he hoped to be up and running by late fall YR-3.

Elliot said he needed someone who could act as his Vice President for Purchasing. He said the job involved buying all the products and services that Minicom needed. He said he thought of me because of my knowledge of computers and because of my business school and law school experience. He thought I would be a great contracting agent for his company. I reminded Elliot about my bad checks problem, which he knew all about from one night in the summer of YR-4 while we were on vacation when I had a bunch to drink and confided in him. Elliot said that he knew who I was at heart, that he trusted me, and that if he had any problems with the conviction, he would not have made the offer.

Elliot also told me that he had persuaded people he knew from previous experiences to join the management team. Charles Bentley from MIT was the VP for Manufacturing; Debbie Silver, whom Zoe knew from her Wall Street days, was the CFO and VP for Finance; and Larry Schwartz, whom Elliot met at NotYours, Inc., was the VP for Marketing.

Elliot said that he had decided to use his cash-out from NotYours and some of Zoe's bonus money from Wall Street to build a future for his family. I later learned that he also got a line of credit for financing based on guarantees from his parents and Zoe's folks. Ellen joined us when Zoe got on the phone, and we found out Zoe was pregnant with their first child, who was due in late July YR-3. We couldn't have been happier for them, and about a month later, when Ellen got her offer from Nita University Memorial, we decided to make the move to Nita City.

I was very much looking forward to the Minicom job. The way Elliot had set up the company, all the VPs came on for a base salary of $45,000 per year. The other VPs took a pay cut, but because I was biding time waiting for Ellen's career move when the offer came in, it was actually a $10,000 raise for me over my Verizon job, but not what I could have earned on the open market. In addition to the base salary, Elliot created a profit-sharing plan whereby he would receive 60 percent of the profits of the business, each VP would receive a guarantee of 5 percent of the profits, and the remainder of the profits would be divided by all the employees of the company (VPs included) based on their years of service at Minicom. Elliot also anticipated that at some point Minicom would go public, and there would be stock options for the four VPs.

We moved to our current condo when Ellen's appointments started in June YR-3. The down payment was a gift from Ellen's parents. The renovations on the Science Drive facility took longer than expected, which delayed the official opening of the business. Elliot continued to work on his designs and demo models for the CyberShield out of his home. He shared with me his work and, although I had been out of the computer business for several years, I could understand, appreciate, and even make some suggestions on his designs. That process also got me up to snuff on the tech knowledge I would need in my job. Debbie, Larry, and Charles delayed their move to Nita City until we opened up in January YR-2. I spent that summer and fall doing some minor renovations on the condo. I also spent time with Elliot, as I said, at his house talking about Minicom and admiring his and Zoe's new son, Jake, who was born in late July. I even did some babysitting, both on my own and with Ellen. We wanted to eventually start a family and Jake was a great advertisement for parenthood.

When we opened in January, Charles and Elliot spent time working on design and demo models, while Debbie set up the financial side of the business and Larry started working on marketing plans. As work progressed, Elliot hired people as needed in the manufacturing/assembly plant, which was also located at the Science Drive location. We now have a total work staff, including the VPs and Elliot, of twenty-two people. all of whom are Nita residents. Elliot considered manufacturing outside the country but fear of theft of his designs and a preference for hiring locals kept those jobs at the Science Drive facility.

My job was to buy all necessary supplies for Minicom. I worked with vendors buying everything from office supplies and desks to computer parts and other items necessary for assembling CyberShield products. I also spent some time getting to know the industry. Our personal cybersecurity products were unique, but they were assembled with parts manufactured by much larger companies; BMI was one of those providers.

Because of our size, we had no written procedure for how orders of products were made at Minicom, so I sort of figured it out as I went along. The formality of the ordering process

I used depended in large part on the expense involved and the requirements of the suppliers. Relatively inexpensive items like office supplies and the like were typically ordered by phone or email, or sometimes in person.

For more expensive items, like component parts for our demo CyberShield product that cost thousands of dollars, companies seemed to have their own requirements, but were not universal. Some suppliers required use of online or hard copy order forms while others would take an order over the phone or via email as long as there was a written confirmation of the order. The bottom line was that we would conform to the processes expected by the supplier of the products we ordered. Generally, it is fair to say that for most suppliers, the formality of the process lessened with the frequency of purchases by us.

The only firm policy Minicom had was that on any purchase over $2,500 shipped to us we required "risk of loss" insurance to protect us against the shipment being lost or damaged in transit to us. I would request the supplier to procure the insurance either as a "shipment policy" or, in the case of shippers such as UPS, by declaring what is called "excess valuation" for the shipment, which meant that they automatically provided and charged for insurance.

We needed shipment insurance or excess valuation declarations because shippers all limit their liability by the terms of their shipping contract. Given the size and number of shipments we were receiving, we had insufficient volume as of the summer and even into the fall of YR-2 to procure an insurance policy that would automatically insure all our orders.

Elliot was initially surprised to learn that the buyer was responsible for lost shipments, which is a matter of Nita law, and that we purchased the insurance on shipments mentioned above. I know I advised Elliot that once we got into a major production run, we should look into what is commonly known as a "blanket" risk-of-loss shipping insurance policy, which covers all incoming shipments on which the insured bears the "risk of loss." He never acted on my advice until February YR-1.

By the late summer of YR-2, Larry Schwartz had procured several orders for our basic product, CyberShield Prime, and was looking for a major retailer for our product. Up until then, we had been purchasing the component parts for our CyberShield Prime demo models from independent jobbers or middlemen because we had no need for the volume required for purchases directly from parts manufacturers , which typically required orders in excess of a gross (144 items). In August of YR-2, in anticipation of our first major production run of CyberShield Prime, Elliot asked me to order a number of the component parts used in our product in amounts sufficient to fill our order. That kind of bulk purchasing allowed me to go directly to the manufacturers and get much better pricing on the parts than we were receiving from the middlemen.

One component we needed in high volume was a graphene interlaced chip platform, usually referred to as an ICP. Manufacturers of ICPs typically sell them in minimum lots of one gross. In our base model CyberShield, two ICPs are used in each unit. For that first production run, which was for a little over 6,000 units, we ordered 100 gross of the ICPs to account for faulty platforms or damage in storage or assembly. Because I had been surveying the potential suppliers for known component parts, I knew that there were not many companies that manufactured ICPs. BMI was one of those suppliers, and in fact they had sent us a brochure and a price list for ICPs earlier in the summer of YR-2. Exhibit 1A is the price list BMI emailed to me.

When I started calling about the pricing and availability of product, I found that the pricing for the part we needed (ICPs come with differing technical characteristics) was remarkably similar across suppliers. The last supplier I contacted was BMI, and I was directed by their information line to their closest distribution facility, which was in Brookline, Massachusetts. The person I spoke with at BMI was Chris Kay. That was on September 3, YR-2. Exhibit 2 is a printout of my computerized phone log that shows that call. We had a policy at Minicom to fill out phone logs for all outgoing and incoming calls on a form on our computers. The data was filled in and stored electronically. The way I filled out the outgoing log was to input the date, the person or company called, and the phone number as I was calling, and then fill in the business purpose column either while on the phone (I use a headset at work to keep my hands free) or right after the call. This log gives us a reliable record of our calls and their content, maintained for any necessary reference.

Kay and I spoke about the technical requirements that we had for ICPs, and we determined that the platform we needed to order was BMI's part number ICP-73. Kay quoted a price of $5,000 per gross, which was acceptable to us, and confirmed that he had 100 gross available for immediate shipment.

Because BMI had the earliest availability and everyone's prices seem to be pretty much the same, I decided to go with BMI. Kay and I talked about the terms of the order and agreed to the price for 100 gross that he quoted, that the parts would be shipped within ten days via NPS, that BMI would procure shipment insurance or declare excess valuation, and that the payment terms would include a discount of 2 percent for payment within thirty days.

Once we had reached an agreement, Kay thanked me for my order, but said that he needed a confirming letter attached to an email, USPS, or other delivery company such as UPS. He also pointed out that their price list had a link that would take me to BMI's online order form.

I was more than willing to provide him with the writing, and decided that, given this was our first order, I wanted to spell out the terms and conditions that we had agreed to in our phone call in a letter. Kay said that was my choice, but encouraged me to use the online order form, at least in the future.

Exhibits 3A and B are the email (Exhibit 3A) with attached letter (Exhibit 3B) that I sent. Exhibit 3C appears to be the letter I mailed. Why they wanted the same letter twice was lost on me but I went along with their request for confirmation of the order I made over the phone. We received the parts, and according to Elliot and Charles Bentley, they were technically acceptable with a very low defect rate. Kay sent me an email with an attached letter and statement of account for the September order. Exhibit 5A is the email, 5B the attached letter, and 5C the attached statement of account. We paid the invoice by check in time to receive the discount. Exhibit 7A is my cover letter that I sent with the check, a copy of which is Exhibit7B.

That was the last I had to do with BMI until January YR-1. BMI did, however, invite Elliot and Zoe to an all-expense paid exposition at Hilton Head, South Carolina, in December of YR-2. Elliot got back from the expo about the time I was leaving for a holiday break, so I didn't really get a chance to talk to him, but I did get an email from him telling me to make another order of ICPs from BMI after the first of the year. Exhibit 11 is a printout of that email.

Larry Schwartz had persuaded Neiman Marcus to order 5,000 units of CyberShield Prime, which used three ICPs per unit. Together with what was left over from the first ICP order, I determined we needed another 100 gross of platforms. Elliot also said in the email that Kay had told him that there was an industry-wide price hike of 10 percent coming in March YR-1 and asked that I check out a rumor he had heard about a price-fixing investigation he thought might be involved in the price hike.

I had read about the price hike, which was due to some materials costs increases, but when I called the Department of Justice and the Federal Trade Commission in early January to check out the rumor, their information officers would neither confirm nor deny that there was an ongoing investigation. Exhibit 15 is my phone log showing my call that day. I will say that they didn't seem surprised by the question, so I assumed there was one going on, but as far as I know nothing came of the investigation.

I returned from my holiday break right before New Year's Day of YR-1. Right after the first of January, I got an email from Elliot informing me that he had purchased a blanket risk-of-loss policy to cover all our incoming shipments based on a tip he got in Hilton Head. Exhibit 12 is a printout of that email. I guess he forgot that I had suggested we investigate blanket policies as early as the fall of YR-3 when we started making bulk orders of component parts for our CyberShield Prime. I was a little surprised that he purchased the policy himself as he usually relies on me to purchase services as well as products, but it's his company, and he can do what he wants. The policy was not going into effect until February 1, so I continued our policy of insuring purchases individually until then.

On January 3, YR-1, I sent an email to Kay at BMI inquiring about another shipment of ICP-73s. Exhibit 13 is a printout of that email. I wanted to find out about availability of the platforms and confirm the price and shipping conditions that were available in September YR-2. By shipping conditions, I meant shipment within ten days, using NPS, and with insurance. Kay didn't respond, but a Virginia Young did on his behalf. Exhibit 14 is a printout of that response. She apparently hadn't read my email carefully because she didn't address the shipping conditions at all, but I knew I would eventually speak or write to Kay to make sure BMI understood our needs.

On January 6, YR-1, I placed a call to Kay. A person identifying herself as Virginia Young and as being Kay's assistant answered the phone. I assumed it was the same Virginia Young who had responded to my email. It turned out that Kay wasn't available to take my call, so I gave our order to Young, telling her I wanted 100 gross of ICP-73s for $500,000, that I wanted them shipped within ten days by NPS, and that I wanted them insured. She said that was fine and asked for a confirming order form. Exhibit 15 is a printout of my computerized phone log for January 6, YR-1, that has the entry for that call. I also asked Young to have Kay give me a call, and she took my phone number. Kay never called.

Within an hour, I used the link to BMI's online order form and filled it out (Exhibit 17C). Because I wanted the order to be handled the same as our first, I wrote in the Special Requirements box that I was confirming order with Young and to "Please handle as per the usual agreement." I also I emailed Kay and attached the order form (as I had done the previous September) confirming the agreement I had made with BMI. I had looked at their order form online, but it wasn't clear to me who would receive the order—it might just go to a warehouse foreman, and since I had discussed the order with Virginia Young I wanted to be sure the order went through Kay's office. I referred specifically to the phone call agreement with Young in the email (Exhibit 17A). Exhibit 17B is the attached letter that I sent making the order. To be clear about what I wanted, I specifically referred to my call with Young and our agreement on the phone. On both the order form and in the email, I stated that I wanted the order to be handled as per the usual agreement we had with BMI, which included insurance. We had only one other agreement, so I don't know how they screwed up and didn't take out insurance.

I did get an email with an attached letter signed by Young for Kay and the invoice a few days later on January 10, YR-1 (Exhibits 19A, 19B, and 19C). Whether I opened the attachment and reviewed the invoice carefully or not the day it came in, I can't say. The email asked to be sure the parts were satisfactory. Since we hadn't gotten them by the time of the email, I could not respond at that time. I probably didn't even get to the account statement. Several days later we got a package from BMI. The shipping record (Exhibit 21) showed that it contained ten gross of ICP-73s, but they were actually ICP-22s. When I sent that mistaken order back to BMI, I insured the parts (Exhibit 22A) and sent a letter explaining the reason for the return. I attached the corrected bill, noting in the letter that BMI had failed to charge us for insurance (Exhibit 22B). I also told Kay in the letter that we really needed the shipment by January 31, YR-1, to fill our Neiman Marcus order.

A few days later, I got an email from Kay saying that the ICP-73s we had ordered were sent out on January 17 and that he was tracing the order with NPS (Exhibit 23). He did not mention anything about the fact they had not billed us for insurance or anything about getting the parts to us by January 31, when they were needed. I texted Elliot about the shipping delay and he responded in kind to keep him informed. Those texts are Exhibits 24 and 25.

The second week in February, Elliot told me that we were running low on ICPs, and I told him that the shipment was still not in, but Kay was looking into it. I remember calling

Kay's office from home at least four times because I was out with the flu, but he did not respond to me. On February 18, YR-1, I got a Fed Ex letter from Kay (Exhibit 26A) saying that NPS had lost the parts. The letter contained a $400 NPS check (Exhibit 26B), which he said was NPS's limit of liability. He also said that he could fill another order of ICPs. I immediately called Kay and asked him whether the shipment insurance on the shipment had paid BMI for the lost parts or whether the insurance check would come to us. Kay said there was no insurance and that we hadn't asked for insurance. I was adamant that we had and went over the phone call with his assistant and the confirming letter. He said there was nothing he could do. Exhibit 27A is a printout of my phone log that records that call.

Yes, I am on medication today. My family doctor renewed my prescription for Lexapro in February YR-1. I take it for anxiety during periods when I am under a lot of stress. Yes, I do have the prescription with me. Okay, now Exhibit 27B is a copy of my prescription label. The last time that I used the Lexapro before BMI lost the shipment was around the time that my store was going out of business and I had that trouble with the law. I did start taking it again since Kay's call. This whole BMI mess has had me very worried. No, I was not taking Lexapro when I made the order of ICPs from BMI in January. I stopped taking it shortly after we moved to Nita City, and even though my work at Minicom was challenging, it wasn't stressing me out. Even if I had been, Lexapro does not affect my ability to function at a high level at my job; in fact, when I am anxious it helps me concentrate. I do not experience drowsiness or any other side effect that interferes with my normal functioning.

After Kay's call, I reviewed my phone log, emails, and correspondence about the order. I was convinced that BMI had screwed up our order. Elliot was out of the office, so I sent him an email suggesting that since he had dealt with Kay personally in Hilton Head that perhaps he could get Kay to replace the shipment that they had failed to insure. Exhibit 28 is a printout of that email. Elliot reviewed my records and agreed that it was a BMI screw-up. I know that he called Kay and was hopeful that the parts would be replaced, but Kay eventually refused to do so. That was sometime after the first week of March.

Once Elliot heard that BMI was not going to make good on their mistake, Elliot told me to order the replacement ICPs from another supplier. I did so from Exrox. Exhibit 33 is a copy of my email ordering those parts. Exhibits 34A, and B are Exrox's email acknowledgement of the order and their bill. Exhibit 37 is a second bill we got from them when we were unable to make timely payment to them.

We had some problems with the Exrox platform. They were configured in a slightly different way than BMI's parts and that required some minor, but necessary, design modifications. That, in addition to BMI's screw up, further delayed the production of our order for Neiman Marcus, so they pulled the plug on the deal when we couldn't deliver their entire order by their April 1 deadline.

I'll admit that I felt very bad that all of this happened and that for a while in March YR-1 I was having some problems at work. I even considered leaving Minicom and made a few inquiries. At some point in early April, Elliot came down to see me and told me to get over it, that we would make do, but that if my work didn't get back to normal that he would have to replace me. I'm happy to say that I've been able to get back to normal and that business seems to be picking up again. I can't say whether we will turn a profit this year; that would be a question for Elliot or Debbie Silver. I do know that we are not so flush that the $500,000 BMI is suing us for wouldn't really hurt.

Statement of Elliot Milstein[4]
August 17, YR-1

I'm Elliot Milstein. I am thirty-two years old. I've been married to Zoe Green for ten years. Our son Jake is two years old. Zoe and I met in high school in Nita City, although we didn't date then. I was a quiet and nerdy and spent a lot of time in the computer lab. Zoe was social and outgoing and a class officer, one of the cool kids. Our only connection was we were both members of the National Honor Society and our grades had us tied for valedictorian. At graduation we gave a joint speech she wrote. We became a couple when we were in college, she at Harvard and me at MIT. We ran into each other in a coffee shop in Harvard Square. One thing led to another; we started dating and fell in love. I think we were the surprise couple at our fifth high school reunion. In YR-10, she graduated from Harvard and I graduated from MIT. We were married that summer. We live at 32 Whitehead Circle in Nita City, Nita.

My undergraduate degree at MIT was in computer science. After graduation, I stayed on at MIT for a computational science and engineering PhD program, graduating in YR-7. While I was doing that, Zoe worked for a financial services firm in Boston and then returned to Harvard for her MBA.

In YR-7, I took a job in applied computing with a startup company called NotYours, Inc. in New York. NotYours was working on rudimentary intra-office computer security problems in the workplace. I was mainly in research and development. I liked the job initially because I was given a good deal of independence and as a startup—although the pay was not great—the company offered stock options at a generous rate. Zoe stayed in Cambridge for her MBA and I commuted back to Boston from Brooklyn on the weekends. After she got her MBA in YR-5, she went to work as a financial analyst on Wall Street. I enjoyed my time at NotYours, Inc. and they achieved some good success in workplace computer security. After a few years, though, I began to think about leaving. The company was not interested in moving on to an area of my personal interest, personal cybersecurity. More importantly, after getting some rave reviews in a couple trade magazines and a write up in the *Wall Street Journal*, the board seemed to decide the sky was the limit. They did two stock splits, and the stock price took off—you'd think none of them remembered the Internet bubble. By late YR-4, I was nervous about the future of the company and ready to move on. I wanted to develop products for use in personal computing and telephone cybersecurity. I considered taking a job with companies in that field, but after lots of late night talks with Zoe, we decided to take the plunge and start our own company. In the end, that choice was consistent with the fact that Zoe and I wanted to start a family and I wanted to be my own boss. I cashed in my NotYours stock options at the end of YR-4, when there was speculation that NotYours would be bought by a Japanese conglomerate and the stock price went through the roof.

---

4. Witnesses should follow this statement as closely as possible, but testify spontaneously. If necessary, witnesses may make up information that they believe is consistent with the witness statement. If there is a material misstatement when compared to what is provided, defending counsel must take reparative action.

In January YR-3, Zoe and I moved back to Nita City to be closer to both Zoe's parents and siblings and my parents so our kids would have their aunts, uncles, cousins, and grandparents in their lives. Both sets of our parents still live in downtown Nita City. I have no siblings, but Zoe has three older sisters, all of whom are married with kids and live in Nita City's suburbs. Zoe's sisters had all taken some time away from their careers to start their families, but by then Myra, a school principal married to a banker; Leslie, a research chemist for Nita Biotechnics married to a lawyer; and Katie, an art gallery manager married to a graphic artist, were back in the workforce.

Zoe and I formed Minicom, Inc. in January YR-3, with us as the sole owners. As it turned out, I was right about NotYours; by late summer YR-3, they were out of business. It was fortunate we decided to make the move when we did. By March YR-3, I finished designing a prototype of a personal cybersecurity product we now call "CyberShield Prime." I had worked on the design on my own time in my final two months at NotYours. I had time for it because I took my accumulated vacation and personal time. I gave the company notice I was leaving on January 1, YR-3, right after I got my YR-4 bonus.

While I was at NotYours—and becoming disenchanted with the work and lack of vision for the future—I started thinking about a personal cybersecurity product I could, in my own company, bring to a very competitive market. Working on CyberShield, I narrowed my focus to cybersecurity devices designed as products to be used with other existing technologies (iPhones, Android phones, and personal computers) as protection from hackers and other cyber thieves. The CyberShield product works with cellphones to protect them from intrusions. It's a thin jacket on the back of a phone that gets charged when the phone is charged on a wireless charger. It connects to the phone through Bluetooth, and it monitors all incoming signals that are not phone calls. If it detects an attempt to access any stored data other than through keystroke input on the phone or direct voice command, it blocks the attempt and sets off an audio and tactile alarm on the phone.

This kind of product was impossible before interlaced graphene computing platforms (known as ICPs) came onto the market. ICPs create exponentially more programmable computing power on a thinner chip, allowing for an add-on device light enough to use with a cellphone.

The first prototype, CyberShield Prime, worked with iPhone's latest model and Android phones. Although I was very interested in starting my own company, I can envision selling the company and the technology we've developed to a major supplier of computer devices in the future.

By the time my prototype was finished, Zoe was pregnant with Jake and not working. She created a business plan for the manufacture, assembly, and marketing of my product. We decided that rather than taking it to a large manufacturer, we should use our own company, Minicom, to produce and market our CyberShield. "Minicom" really didn't describe our product but I had the rights to the name, URL, and other important intangible assets. We extended the company name to Minicom: Personal Cyber Security. No, I didn't update the name with the Secretary of State's business office. It's still just Minicom, Inc., legally.

Our personal cybersecurity startup was now ready to become operational. My NotYours stock options funded the business, combined with most of our savings, which had come largely from Zoe's bonuses from her jobs in the finance industry. We also obtained a substantial line of credit with the Nita National Bank based on guarantees signed by both sets of parents. By March YR-3, my plans were coming together. I found a warehouse on Science Drive in the Nita Research Park that was the right size for my operation, but it needed renovation. The lessor agreed to make the renovations according to my specifications. I signed a long-term lease and began renovating. Zoe and I also assembled our management team.

Zoe and I were interested in bringing people we liked to the company, people who would invest their time and talent in a new enterprise as a bet on our future success. We were looking for four management-level people, our "vice presidents." Debbie Silver was a friend and coworker of Zoe's from Wall Street. She was also a specialist in taking companies public, which was and is our long-term goal for Minicom. Looking for a new challenge, she came aboard as the CFO and VP for Finance. Larry Schwartz had worked as a marketing manager at NotYours and was my closest friend from there. He cashed out when I did and was on board with our product goals. He became our VP for Marketing and Sales. Charles Bentley was a friend from the MIT graduate program. He was disenchanted with the large companies he had been working with; he came on as our VP for Manufacturing. These people all took real pay cuts—we pay $45,000 a year and a portion of profits, and stock options if we went public, which, as I said is our plan.

The last position we needed to fill was for a contracting/purchasing agent for the company. We called the position VP for Purchasing. My oldest and best friend from MIT is Mike Lubell. He was my undergraduate roommate. During college, Zoe introduced Mike to his now-wife, Ellen, who was a college classmate of hers at Harvard, and we have been close to them since then. While we were still in the Boston area, we would see Mike and Ellen at least two or three times a month. After we moved away, we mostly communicated by phone and email, but we vacationed together for a week each summer at the New Jersey shore.

Mike was a computer science major at MIT. While not the best student—probably because he wasn't as interested in the curriculum as he might have been—Mike was bright, articulate, and intellectually facile and curious, with varied interests and a lot of info about a lot of things.

After graduating from MIT, Mike thought that business school would interest him. He enrolled in Boston University's MBA program when they decided that his computer expertise could serve as a waiver for the normal two years' experience in the financial industry for applicants to the program. I know he did well in his first year, but that summer he decided that he wasn't interested in a Wall Street career and left the program. For the next year he worked at the Genius Bar at an Apple store while he applied to law school. He eventually was accepted at Northeastern and started law school in YR-8.

Almost from the beginning he disliked law school. Because he was bright, he did well his first year, but he decided that life as a law student was not for him. He must have learned something, however, because he went to work as a paralegal for a large law firm in Boston that did patent work. In that way he used both his MIT and law school learning in his work.

Mike told me he was only doing the job because the pay was good, and he needed to help support Ellen's education (she was in med school at Tufts).

There was one potential problem with Mike that Zoe and I struggled with. In late spring YR-6, Mike was approached by a friend of his from business school, John Staffier, to go in with him on a retail electronic gaming shop in Cambridge, which they called Techno-Toys. Although I felt that Mike could have done better than running a games store, he seemed to enjoy his work and the independence it gave him. The store, which had a great location near thousands of undergraduate students, did very well until the fall of YR-5, when a big box electronics store opened in the area, selling many of the same products as Techno-Toys with a volume discount. It ran Mike and John out of business. They closed and went into bankruptcy in January YR-4.

That process was hard on Mike. He had been desperate to save his business. I later learned that to pay for a critical order near the end, he wrote personal checks and they bounced. He was so embarrassed he didn't ask Ellen or anyone else to help cover them and before he knew it, he had been arrested. I wish Mike had come to me. The checks totaled only a thousand dollars, and we would have lent it to him, but he was too proud. I didn't discover his problems with the law until our Jersey Shore vacation that summer. Mike and I were up late with a little too much to drink and he unburdened himself. I also know that he made good on every check because it was the right thing to do.

Zoe and I knew that when Ellen finished her fellowship at Massachusetts General Hospital in YR-3, the Lubells' next move would be governed by where Ellen wanted to start her practice. Because of that uncertainty, Mike couldn't get a career-oriented job, so he worked at the Verizon store in a local mall doing retail sales while waiting for Ellen to finish her program.

Both Zoe and I thought that Mike would be perfect as our VP for Purchasing. He knew the basic technical aspects of digital equipment design necessary to procure parts, and he had graduate work in business and law, which we thought would serve him well as Minicom's contracting agent. No, I was not concerned about the bad checks situation. That was old news, and clearly an aberration.

In February YR-3, we called Mike and Ellen to tell them about our pregnancy. We offered Mike the VP for Purchasing position in the same call. The timing was perfect because Ellen was interviewing for her next career move, and we knew that the University of Nita Medical School and Nita Memorial Hospital were on her list. When I told Mike about our plans, about the VPs we had taken on, and asked him to join us, he said "yes" immediately, contingent on Ellen getting a position in Nita City. When Ellen accepted a clinical position at Nita Memorial and a faculty job at Nita University Med School, Mike signed on. Ellen's position started in June YR-3, and they moved into a condo at that time.

The renovations on the Science Drive facility were going slowly, so Minicom did not officially open until January YR-2. Mike kept himself busy renovating the condo he and Ellen bought. He also spent time overseeing the Minicom renovations and talking with me about Minicom and our new product, CyberShield. His design suggestions, although not very sophisticated regarding computer science, helped me with practical use issues, and our conversations helped me. At the same time, he was getting current on the design of our product, which was necessary in making component part purchases. When Jake was born on July 22, YR-3, Mike and Ellen adored him. Mike did some babysitting when Zoe and I needed a break.

When the renovation finally was completed in December YR-3, we set the formal opening date at January 3, YR-2. Debbie, Larry, and Charles moved to Nita City right around then, and we opened. At first, the only people working were the five of us on the management team and two administrative assistants, whom we shared. As I said, the management team recognized our startup situation, and all agreed to draw a salary of only $45,000 each per year with profit sharing and a promise of stock options if things worked as we planned.

For everyone except Mike, who had last worked at Verizon, the salary was much lower than what they had been making. But the way we set up Minicom, it had potential for large financial rewards for all of us, if the business took off and went public. The deal before them was that when we were profitable, each of the VPs would receive 5 percent of the profit; another 20 percent would be shared by Minicom's employees (including the VPs) according to a formula based solely on their years of service at Minicom. The remaining 60 percent would go to me and Zoe. We have added employees as necessary; our total workforce, including management, is now twenty-two people, most of whom work assembling our products. And yes, we considered having all the work done overseas, but we were concerned about technology theft and wanted to create jobs in Nita City.

During the spring and early summer of YR-2, Charles and I worked on finalizing my designs and building the final basic version of CyberShield. Debbie set up the company's finances. Mike made sure we had the materials for our first production run, buying literally every product and service we needed. Larry finalized marketing plans for our products.

Larry's marketing efforts succeeded, and in late summer YR-2, we had contracts to provide 6,000 of our basic CyberShield units to various mobile phone retailers in time for Christmas. Until the summer of YR-2, we had been purchasing relatively small quantities of the parts we needed from jobbers as our designs evolved. That summer I learned from a friend in the computer industry that we could get enormous savings by purchasing parts directly from manufacturers, who required the larger bulk orders that we now needed.

A key part in our CyberShields is the interlaced graphene computing platform, known in the industry as an ICP. It's an addressable, programable mini-computer on a tiny platform. Once we had our orders in place, I asked Mike to investigate purchasing ICPs in bulk, as well as other components for the production run of our base unit CyberShield Prime product.

After some checking around, Mike confirmed prices per unit were lower for bulk purchases and learned that the ICPs, for example, were normally sold in lots of one gross. A gross is

144 parts. Because each of the 6,000 base model CyberShield Primes in our first order utilized two ICPs per unit, we purchased 100 gross to account for part failure and damage during assembly or storage. We eventually chose BMI as our ICP supplier and ordered 100 gross of their ICP-73 for $500,000 in early September YR-2. The parts were received promptly and were of exceptional quality.

In November YR-2, I got a call from a Chris Kay, who identified himself as the BMI sales manager who had dealt with us in our ICP order. Exhibit 8 is my phone log showing that call. At Minicom, all the managers keep a digital log of incoming and outgoing phone calls. It's one of the few set procedures we have and it ensures we have decent records of oral business communications. When he called, Kay invited me to a BMI Expo in Hilton Head, South Carolina, in December. He explained that it was an all-expense paid trip for me and a guest, and that besides getting to meet other people in the electronics industry, there would be plenty of time for recreation. I accepted the invitation for two reasons. First, Zoe and I had not had a vacation since Jake had been born. Second, at Minicom we were long on enthusiasm, but short on business experience. I thought it was important for me to learn what I could from such an opportunity. At first my main responsibility at Minicom was on the technical end but, as time went on, I needed a better understanding of the computer industry.

The Hilton Head trip was very pleasant. The weather was a lot better than in Nita City, and we got in some fishing, beach walking, and golf, all of which we enjoyed. I also got to meet several people in the electronics business. Some were relative newcomers like me, working in startup companies, but others were very experienced and working in well-established companies. And there were the BMI people, who seemed genuinely interested in developing a good relationship with us.

Kay shepherded us for much of the Expo. Apparently, Minicom is in his region for BMI. Although he was obviously there to hustle more business, he seemed to be a friendly and knowledgeable guy. We had lots of talks about business, generally, but two pieces of information stayed with me. The first tip was that a materials cost increase to manufacturers was about to cause an industry-wide price hike of 10 percent for ICPs in March YR-1. The second tip related to the insurance policy we purchased for the September shipment of ICPs. I knew we did that because we always insure incoming shipments over $2,500 in value against loss or damage in transit. Mike had told me that in our business, different from consumer transactions, lost shipments were the responsibility of the buyer, not the seller. According to Mike, even though it didn't make a lot of sense to me, losses and damage by the shipper were limited by law and were the responsibility of the buyer, as opposed to the seller. Kay's tip was to get what he called a "blanket risk-of-loss" insurance policy to cover all our incoming shipments. Apparently, the insurer charges for that quarterly, based on the audited value of the incoming shipments. Kay said that was how most companies covered themselves and that it was much less expensive than the single shipment insurance policies we were using. I am always interested in saving money, so I made a mental note to investigate a policy when I returned to Nita City. I told Kay I would look into it, but I never told him I was definitely going to do it because I had no idea what it would cost.

I do remember Kay mentioning we had used emailed letters to make our September order, as opposed to the BMI online order form, which he recommended. To be honest I didn't give it another thought. So long as letters worked, I could see no reason to change what we were doing to make their job easier.

When I got back home, I told Mike about the price hike. I was a little surprised he didn't know about it, given it was industry-wide. I also told him there was a rumor at my gym that BMI was under investigation for antitrust violations and asked Mike to see if the price hike was related to the investigation. I also made appointments with insurance brokers for after the first of the year to price blanket insurance policies. The only reason I investigated it myself was that I was curious about how that part of our business worked. Normally this is something Mike would handle. As far as I know, Mike was not aware that such a thing existed; not to say he didn't, but we never spoke about that insurance as far as I recall. If Mike says we did, I wouldn't argue with him, but it obviously did not make an impression on me.

I spoke with agents in January YR-1 and purchased a blanket risk-of-loss policy that became effective on February 1, YR-1, and covered all our incoming shipments. Kay was right; the policy should save us about $20,000 per year once we are functional. I informed Mike of the policy purchase by email and reminded him to get shipment policies on incoming purchases through the end of January. Exhibit 12 is a printout of that email.

By the end of YR-2, our balance sheet showed we were breaking even. We were making enough to cover expenses and salaries. Though we had no profit in YR-2, we lost nothing either; we were very hopeful of turning a profit in YR-1. That was especially so because we got a good reaction to our base model CyberShield Primes sold in YR-2, and because we had an order from Neiman Marcus for 5,000 of our CyberShield Primes to be delivered to them in April of YR-1, in time for their summer catalogue. The Neiman Marcus order was important for us because it was the first sale of our more sophisticated units, which we thought would impress the market. The profit margin was relatively low on this first order ($20 per unit), but the prospect of a $100,000 profit was encouraging and made it likely that we would be profitable for YR-1. The Neiman Marcus buyer, Greg Smith, told me that given the positive customer reaction, he expected that they would order another 15,000 units for October YR-1 delivery; and assuming we kept up with tech developments (which was our strong suit), yearly orders in the 20,000 unit range or more were virtually assured. He said their typical contract was for three years. Exhibit 10 is my phone log for that conversation. I knew how good our product was, so I was confident about the additional orders and expected they might even be larger than called for in the contract. I also thought that Nieman might be interested in upgrading to our CyberShield Platinum units, then under development.

At any rate, Prime units each required four ICPs. We had only several thousand ICPs left over at the end of YR-2, so we needed the January YR-1 order from BMI to assemble the Prime models for Neiman's. I had told Mike about this in December YR-2. The Neiman Marcus order was important to us because they reach the market most inclined to be interested in our highest end (and most profitable) products.

The Neiman Marcus deal, beyond the first shipment, was never signed because when BMI lost our parts and wouldn't replace them in time, we couldn't meet our April 1, YR-1, deadline. Neiman Marcus pulled the plug on the order. Greg said he was sorry it didn't work out, but timing was everything for them; given that most of their sales of electronics were made via the Internet or through catalogues, they depended on timely shipment. He also said he went to bat for me but the people in charge insisted on absolute adherence to schedules. Just last month, in July YR-1, Larry tried to get their business again, but Greg Smith told him they required absolute certainty on timing so, against his recommendation—he believed our product was superior, but the company was more interested in consistency—Nieman signed an exclusive contract with one of our competitors for three years.

I didn't have anything to do with the January order from BMI until February YR-1, when I texted Mike about our urgent need for the platforms. He texted back that there was a problem with the shipment, but Kay was working on it. I was returning from a long weekend with friends when I got Mike's email saying that BMI's shipment was lost, and that even though he had requested insurance, Kay denied that the request was made and had said the loss was our problem (Exhibit 28).

Back in the office, I looked over Mike's phone log, emails, and letters, and agreed with him that he had requested insurance. At Mike's suggestion I called Kay to see if I could work something out with him. My phone log is Exhibit 29. Kay was very apologetic over the phone and said that he would look into replacing the shipment at no cost to us. He made no promises, but he did say he would do his best for us with his legal department, that we were an important client, and that he wanted to have a long-term relationship with us. I also told him we needed the parts to complete our Neiman Marcus order, which was very important to us. Kay said he understood, and I was optimistic that he would make the situation right and replace the ICPs, which BMI had in stock.

Because Kay was involving his lawyers, I made an appointment with our lawyer, and after talking with her, we agreed to wait and see what Kay did, given he had promised a quick response. Kay never even gave me the courtesy of a return phone call. About two weeks later I got a curt letter (Exhibit 30) that read like it was written by a lawyer, basically telling us to get lost and demanding that we pay for parts we never got. I'll admit I was angry, especially because Kay was so positive in our phone call and then so rude as to not even return the call. Annoyed, I wrote him a not very nice letter (Exhibit 31). We never paid for those platforms because it was BMI's responsibility to provide us with insurance, and they failed to do so. The next we heard from BMI was when they sued us.

After I got Kay's letter in March, I immediately told Mike to get the parts from another supplier. He did—this time from Exrox. True to Kay's word, the price was 10 percent or $50,000 higher, and because of a slight difference in the configuration of the Exrox part, we had to make a minor design change. The design change would not have been a problem if we'd had the parts in February, but given that BMI didn't deliver what we ordered, then screwed around before finally telling us we were out of luck, and then the design change . . . we lost the Neiman Marcus account for at least three years.

Even though Mike did nothing wrong, he was down in the dumps about the problem with BMI, and for a while he was making mistakes because he was not focusing. I thought some tough love would help him focus so I told him that if he did not snap out of it, I might have to let him go. That seemed to work, and he is doing much better these days. Truth is, I would never fire Mike.

Larry is out every day trying to market our products using traditional techniques and viral marketing on the Internet. We continue to get great technical reviews and are still hoping to break into a larger market, but the Neiman Marcus opportunity was big for us, and it might be quite a while (perhaps years) before we get another good shot at the high-end market, as a stepping stone to places like Costco where the real profit is. Our sales of lower-end CyberShields continue, and if we do not get a bad result in this lawsuit, we should at least break even this year, maybe even make a few bucks. We would have done a hell of a lot better had BMI done what it promised to do.

EXHIBITS

Exhibit 1A

Michael Lubell

From:	customerinfo@bmi.brookline
Sent:	1 Jul YR-2 16:58:16 -0500 (EST)
To:	Michael Lubell <michael@minicom.nita>
Subject:	ICPs for you

BMI

One Industrial Drive
Brookline, MA 02146

Business Machines, Inc.

www.bmi.brookline
(800) BMI-2000
Fax: (800) BMI-2222
Email: info@bmi.brookline

July 1, YR-2

Dear Customer,

Below are our latest prices for interlaced Graphene Computing Platforms. Please note that our price increase is the lowest in the industry. We regret the increases, but higher costs for raw materials made them impossible to avoid.

PART NO.	PRICE PER GROSS
ICP-14	$12,250.00
ICP-22	$11,500.00
ICP-26	$11,000.00
ICP-26A	$11,100.00
ICP-39	$10,800.00
ICP-40	$10,400.00
ICP-51	$ 9,250.00
ICP-52	$ 8,000.00
ICP-65	$ 7,650.00
ICP-73	$ 5,000.00
ICP-80	$ 3,850.00

NOTE:

BMI SELLS THESE PARTS IN LOTS OF ONE GROSS. SMALLER ORDERS WILL NOT BE ACCEPTED.

Payment terms: Cash within sixty days. A 2 percent discount (goods only) is given for prompt payment within thirty days; 1.5 percent per month is charged on accounts not paid within sixty days.

We regret that we cannot accept telephone orders. All orders must be in writing using BMI's order form whether by email, fax, or mail.

Click for Order Form

Exhibit 1B

BMI Business Machines, Inc.

About BMI V Regional Divisions V News V **Online Ordering V** Support V

Company

Contact Person
First Name Last Name

Shipping Address

Email Phone

City State Zip Code

My Order
Item Number Quantity Price Item Total
$0.00

Add item

BMI will ship your order within 10 or less days utilizing NPS or the carrier of your choosing, with all conditions governed by the U.C.C. Please state any special conditions for this order in the space provided.

Comments/Special Instructions

Submit

Payment terms: Cash within sixty days. A 2 percent discount (goods only) is given for prompt payment within thirty days; 1.5 percent per month is charged on accounts not paid within sixty days.

We regret that we cannot accept telephone orders. All orders must be in writing using BMI's order form whether by email or mail.

Exhibit 2

MINICOM

PERSONAL CYBER SECURITY

Employee: Michael Lubell

Call Log | Voicemail | Fax | Settings

Person Called/Calling | Number | Business Purpose

Date	Person Called/ **Calling**	Number	Business Purpose
9/3/YR-2	Acme Café	542-2389	Ordered more cups & stirrers.
9/3/YR-2	Spring Valley Water Co.	682-9002	Ordered add'l supplies and second cooler for employee cafeteria.
9/3/YR-2	Kalo's Katering	887-5387	Ordered lunch for exec. conference.
9/3/YR-2	**Houston Instruments (Mike Jenkins)**		Returned my call about price for ICPs. None available.
9/3/YR-2	Business Machines Inc. (Chris Kay)	800-264-2000	Priced ICPs at 100g. Ordered same at 500K. They will insure at our cost.
9/3/YR-2	9AM Wire (Debbie Burnstein)	783-4636	Ordered 5K feet of CAT5 wire. Same price. They will insure at our cost.

Exhibit 3A

Michael Lubell

From: Michael Lubell <michael@minicom.nita>
Sent: 3 Sep YR-2 2:43:21
To: Chris Kay <chris.kay@bmi.brookline>
Subject: ICP-73 order
Attachment: Order.doc

Mr. Kay,

The letter confirming Minicom's order is attached per our telephone conversation. A hard copy is being sent by USPS.

Michael

Michael Lubell
VP Purchasing Minicom, Inc.
michael@minicom.nita
Direct phone: (819) 555-2188
www.minicom.nita

MINICOM
PERSONAL CYBER SECURITY

Exhibit 3B

MINICOM
PERSONAL CYBER SECURITY

Minicom, Inc.
724 Science Drive
Nita City, Nita 80027

Phone: (819) 555-2122
Fax: (819) 555-2127
www.minicom.nita

September 3, YR-2

VIA EMAIL
Mr. Chris Kay, Sales Manager
Business Machines Incorporated
1 Industrial Drive
Brookline, MA 02146

Dear Mr. Kay:

This is to confirm our phone conversation earlier today in which we agreed to the following transaction. Business Machines Incorporated agrees to sell 100 gross of ICPs (your part no. ICP-73) at $5,000 per gross for a total price of $500,000. Shipment will be made within ten days to our offices via National Parcel Service, and BMI will insure the shipment for full value.

Minicom Incorporated agrees to pay the total purchase price plus shipping and insurance charges. Payment within thirty days after receipt of goods will be credited with a 2 percent discount. Payment between thirty and sixty days after receipt will be for the full price. Payment after sixty days will include a 1.5 percent per month finance charge.

Please notify me if this letter does not conform to your understanding of our agreement.

Yours truly,

s/Michael Lubell

Michael Lubell
Vice President Purchasing
michael@minicom.nita
Direct phone: (819) 555-2188

ML/jaf

Exhibit 3C

MINICOM
PERSONAL CYBER SECURITY

Minicom, Inc.
724 Science Drive
Nita City, Nita 80027

Phone: (819) 555-2122
Fax: (819) 555-2127
www.minicom.nita

September 3, YR-2

VIA U.S. MAIL
Mr. Chris Kay, Sales Manager
Business Machines Incorporated
1 Industrial Drive
Brookline, MA 02146

Dear Mr. Kay:

This is to confirm our phone conversation earlier today in which we agreed to the following transaction. Business Machines Incorporated agrees to sell 100 gross of ICPs (your part no. ICP-73) at $5,000 per gross for a total price of $500,000. Shipment will be made within ten days to our offices via National Parcel Service, and BMI will insure the shipment for full value.

Minicom Incorporated agrees to pay the total purchase price plus shipping and insurance charges. Payment within thirty days after receipt of goods will be credited with a 2 percent discount. Payment between thirty and sixty days after receipt will be for the full price. Payment after sixty days will include a 1.5 percent per month finance charge.

Please notify me if this letter does not conform to your understanding of our agreement.

Yours truly,

Michael Lubell

Michael Lubell
Vice President Purchasing
michael@minicom.nita
Direct phone: (819) 555-2188

ML/jaf

Exhibit 4

Virginia Young

From: Virginia Young, <virginiayoung.2@bmi.brookline>
Sent: Fri, 6 Sep YR-2 13:29:34-0500 (EDT)
To: order_confirm@bmi.brookline
Subject: Work order

Order confirmed today requires shipment immediately of 100 gross of ICP-73 to

Minicom Inc.
724 Science Drive
Nita City, Nita 80027

Ship NPS prepaid insure for 500,000. Shipment Date: 9-6-YR-2 Warehouseman: Tim Groody

Exhibit 5A

Michael Lubell

From:	Virginia Young, <virginiayoung.2@bmi.brookline>
Sent:	Mon, 9 Sep YR-2 10:18:26-0500 (EDT)
To:	Michael Lubell <michael@minicom.nita>
Subject:	Your Sept. 3 Order
Attachments	TY93-001.docx; ST93-001.docx

Please see the attached letter and statement.

Exhibit 5B

BMI

Business Machines, Inc.

One Industrial Drive
Brookline, MA 02146

www.bmi.brookline
(800) BMI-2000
Fax: (800) BMI-2222
Email: info@bmi.brookline

September 9, YR-2

Mr. Michael Lubell
Minicom Incorporated
724 Science Drive
Nita City, NI 80027

Dear Mr. Lubell:

Thank you for your recent first order from Business Machines Incorporated. We hope your purchase represents the beginning of a long and successful business relationship.

As noted in the attached statement of account, we have shipped your goods as per our agreement. Please notify me immediately if the goods are in any way unsatisfactory or if any error appears in your statement.

BMI appreciates your business.

Sincerely,

Chris Kay

Chris Kay Sales Manager
Eastern Subdivision II
chris.kay@bmi.brookline

CK/vy Encl.

Exhibit 5C

BMI

Business Machines, Inc.

One Industrial Drive
Brookline, MA 02146

www.bmi.brookline
(800) BMI-2000
Fax: (800) BMI-2222
Email: info@bmi.brookline

STATEMENT OF ACCOUNT

September 16, YR-2
Minicom Inc.
724 Science Drive
Nita City, NI 80027

Attn: Mr. Michael Lubell

DATE	ITEMS SHIPPED	DEBIT	CREDIT
9/16/YR-2	100 Gross ICP-73	$ 500,000.00	
	Shipping	122.60	
	Insurance	1,110.00	
		Balance due	**$ 501,232.60**

Make all checks payable to Business Machines, Inc.

Accounts paid within thirty days receive a 2 percent discount (goods only) for prompt payment. Full payment is due within sixty days. Interest of 1.5 percent per month will be added to accounts after sixty days.

Exhibit 6

NPS
NATIONAL PARCEL SERVICE

SHIPPING RECORD

SHIPPING RECEIPT—WHITE
NPS COPY—CANARY

RECEIVED FROM

NAME	Business Machines Inc.	DATE	9/9/YR-2
STREET	One Industrial Drive		
CITY/STATE	Brookline, Mass.	ZIP CODE	02146

SEND TO

NAME	MINICOM Inc.		
STREET	724 Science Drive		
CITY/STATE	Nita City, Nita	ZIP CODE	80027

IF COD	DECLARED VALUE	ZONE	
$ ______ AMOUNT	$ ______ AMOUNT	AIR	GROUND STD

PACKAGE CONTENTS

100 GROSS ICP-73

DO NOT WRITE BELOW THIS LINE

TYPE CHARGE	CUSTOMER COUNTER	DATE	TRAN	CHARGES AMOUNT
COD ______	$125,000		Insurance:	$ 1,110
			Shipping	122.60
EXCESS VALUTATION ______				$ 1,232.60
PACKAGE ______	210			

Unless a greater value is declared in writing on this receipt, the shipper hereby declares and agrees that the released value of each package or article not enclosed in a package covered by this receipt is $100, which is a reasonable value under the circumstances surrounding the transportation. The entry of a DOC amount is not a declaration of value. In addition, the maximum value for an air service shipment is $5,000 and the maximum carrier liability is $5,000. Claims not made to carrier within nine months of shipment date are waived. Customer's check accepted at shipper's risk unless otherwise noted on COD tag.

Thank you for using NATIONAL PARCEL SERVICE

Exhibit 7A

MINICOM
PERSONAL CYBER SECURITY

Minicom, Inc.
724 Science Drive
Nita City, Nita 80027

Phone: (819) 555-2122
Fax: (819) 555-2127
www.minicom.nita

September 23, YR-2

Mr. Chris Kay, Sales Manager
Business Machines Incorporated
1 Industrial Drive
Brookline, MA 02146

Dear Mr. Kay:

Thank you for your prompt shipment of ICP-73s. They were received in good order. Enclosed please find our check #2104 in the amount of $491,232.60 representing the purchase price plus shipping and insurance, less the 2 percent ($10,000.00) discount for prompt payment. We look forward to conducting business with you on this basis in the future.

Yours truly,

Michael Lubell

Michael Lubell
Vice President Purchasing
michael@minicom.nita
Direct phone: (819) 555-2188

ML/jaf
Encl.

Exhibit 7B

MINICOM INC.
724 Science Drive
Nita City, Nita 80027
Phone (720) 555-1212

2104

September 23, YR-2

PAY TO THE ORDER OF:

Business Machines Incorporated $ 491,232.60

Four hundred ninety-one thousand two hundred thirty-two and 60/100 DOLLARS

Nita National Bank
Nita City, Nita 80027

Elliot Milstein

*Memo*____________________

ENDORSE CHECK HERE:

PAY TO THE ORDER OF
Business Machines Inc.
NITA NATIONAL BANK
Nita City, Nita 80027
FOR DEPOSIT ONLY
September 30th, Yr-2

Exhibit 8

MINICOM

PERSONAL CYBER SECURITY

Employee: Elliot Milstein

Call Log | Voicemail | Fax | Settings

Person Called/Calling | Number | Business Purpose

Date	Person Called/ **Calling**	Number	Business Purpose
11/12/YR-2	Crot, Watershed Accounting	(819) 555-6753	Discussed preparation for year-end audit.
11/12/YR-2	**Edward Austin Buyer, Staples**		Discussed our new HANDe. Referred call to Larry Schwartz, VP for Sales.
11/12/YR-2	**Chris Kay**		I accepted Expo invite. He will send a formal invitation.
11/12/YR-2	**Joe Kalo**		Wants payment for last executive lunch. Referred to Silver, VP Accounting.
11/12/YR-2	**Greg Smith**		Neiman Marcus follow-up from Larry—Agreed to ship 5,000 units of ACC model HWC by 4/1/YR-1 at $180.00/unit. 10/1—15 k units in October and 20K per year for next two years if quality OK.

Exhibit 9A

Chris Kay

From:	Chris Kay <chris.kay@bmi.brookline>
Sent:	Mon., 18 Nov YR-2 11:22:48 -500 (EST)
To:	Elliot Milstein, <elliot@minicom.nita>
CC:	Virginia Young <virginia.young@bmi.brookline>
Subject:	BMI EXPO
Attachment:	Invitation.docx

Elliot—

I am delighted you and your wife will be able to join us at Hilton Head. Because of the business purpose of the Expo, BMI will, of course, pay all expenses for you and your wife, including airfare. I have taken the liberty of reserving a one-bedroom suite on the golf course for you.

I look forward to seeing you at the Expo and on the golf course. Please notify my assistant, Virginia Young, of both your golf handicaps so we may properly pair you for the tournament.

Chris Kay Sales Manager
Eastern Subdivision II
chris.kay@bmi.nita

Exhibit 9B

Business Machines Incorporated
Requests the pleasure of your company at our
Eastern Regional Exposition of Computer Products
at
The Inn Hilton Head, South Carolina
From Thursday, December 12
through Sunday, December 15, YR-2
R.S.V.P. (800) BMI-2000

Exhibit 10

MINICOM

PERSONAL CYBER SECURITY

Employee: Elliot Milstein

Call Log | Voicemail | Fax | Settings

Person Called/Calling | Number | Business Purpose

Date	Person Called/ Calling	Number	Business Purpose
12/13/YR-2	**Crot, Watershed Accounting**		Reporting status of year-end audit.
12/13/YR-2	Voyager Ins. Co.	819-427-1420	Asked about risk-of-loss insurance. They do not offer.
12/13/YR-2	Vermont General Ins. Co.	802-529-2178	R of L policy not available. Try New Britain L & C.
12/13/YR-2	New Britain Life & Casualty	203-765-2257	They offer policy. Flat premium covers up to $50,000/shipment.
12/13/YR-2	Skipper Ins. Co.	819-422-1925	Same policy will run less than NBL & C. Agent to make appt. to come in after 1st of year.
12/13/YR-2	Kalo's Katering	887-5397	Discussed service at the last exec. lunch. Promises prompt delivery next time.
12/13/YR-2	Neiman Marcus (Greg Smith)	214-323-5974	Confirmed order of 5,000 units HWCs to be delivered no later than April 1, YR-1.

Exhibit 11

Elliot Milstein

From:	Elliot Milstein < elliot@minicom.nita>
Sent:	Sun., 15 Dec YR-2 16:48:22 -700 (MST)
To:	Michael Lubell <michael@minicom.nita>
Subject:	Purchase of ICPs

Before you leave for vacation, I wanted to remind you that we need to place an order for ICPs with BMI for Neiman 5k unit order for April 1—15k potential order on 10/1. The accountants tell me that our cash flow situation will be better after the first of the year, so I suggest that you wait until early January to place the order.

Chris Kay of BMI told me recently that there is an industry-wide price increase of 10 percent coming on March 1. The word at the club is that BMI is in some kind of antitrust trouble with the Justice Department in Washington. You might try to subtly find out if they still plan to go ahead with the price hike.

Exhibit 12

Elliot Milstein

From: Elliot Milstein, < elliot@minicom.nita>
Sent: Fri, 3 Jan YR-1 11:25:10 -0700 (MST)
To: Michael Lubell <michael@minicom.nita>
Subject: Insurance on Purchases/Change in Policy

This is to let you know that today I purchased what is called a blanket risk-of-loss insurance policy to cover all incoming shipments. The purchase was from the Skipper Insurance Company. The policy goes into effect on February 1 of this year. We should continue to follow our standard procedure of insuring all incoming shipments individually until that date. After February 1, all purchases will be insured automatically.

Mike, this is a tip I picked up at Hilton Head. It should save us about $20,000 a year. Looks like this business may make it after all.

Exhibit 13

Michael Lubell

From:	Michael Lubell <michael@minicom.nita>
Sent:	Fri., 3 Jan YR-1 13:15:44 -0700 (MST)
To:	Chris Kay <chris.kay@bmi.brookline>
Subject:	ICP-73 order

Mr. Kay,

Please advise on the availability of 100 gross ICP-73 at $5,000 per gross on the same payment and shipping conditions as our September YR-2 order.

Michael

Michael Lubell
VP Purchasing Minicom, Inc.
michael@minicom.nita
Direct phone: (819) 555-2188
www.minicom.nita

MINICOM
PERSONAL CYBER SECURITY

Exhibit 14

Michael Lubell

From:	Virginia Young virginiayoung.2@bmi.brookline
CC:	order_confirm@bmi.brookline
Sent:	Fri., 3 Jan YR-1 16:58:16 -0500 (EST)
To:	Michael Lubell <michael@minicom.nita>
Subject:	Re: ICP-73 order

Mr. Lubell,

Thank you for your interest in placing an order with us. We have 100 gross ICP-73 in stock for immediate shipment. Price is $500,000 for 100 gross. Payment terms remain same per our price list. Please place your order using our online order form. I will send link if necessary. Alternatively, you may place your order via email or letter.

Virginia Young
BMI
One Industrial Drive
Brookline, MA 02416
(800) BMI-2000

Exhibit 15

MINICOM

PERSONAL CYBER SECURITY

Employee: Michael Lubell

Call Log | Voicemail | Fax | Settings

Person Called/Calling | Number | Business Purpose

Date	Person Called/ Calling	Number	Business Purpose
1/6/YR-1	Kalo's Katering	887-5387	Ordered exec. lunch for today.
1/6/YR-1	Information Officer Justice Dept. Antitrust Div.	202-421-3000	Inquired about BMI antitrust problems. Details not available to public, but officer seemed to know about it.
1/6/YR-1	BMI Chris Kay (spoke to V. Young)	800-264-2000	Ordered 100g ICP-73 at $5,000/g. They will insure at our cost. I will confirm by letter.
1/6/YR-1	Opp's Plumbing	347-2281	Will come 6:30 A.M. tomorrow to repair exec. toilet. Night watchman to be notified.

Exhibit 16

Virginia Young

From:	Virginia Young <virginiayoung.2@bmi.brookline>
Sent:	Mon., 6 Jan YR-1 11:15:26 -0500 (EST)
To:	Chris Kay < chris.kay@BMI.brookline>
Subject:	message

Michael Lubell of Minicom Inc. telephoned about a potential order and would like you to return his call at (819) 555-2188.

Virginia Young
BMI
One Industrial Drive
Brookline, MA 02416
(800) BMI-2000

Exhibit 17A

Michael Lubell

From:	Michael Lubell <michael@minicom.nita>
Sent:	Mon., 6 Jan YR-1 9:37:21 -0700 (MST)
To:	Chris Kay <chris.kay@bmi.brookline>
Subject:	ICP-73 order
Attachment:	Order.doc

Dear Mr. Kay:

This is to confirm my call earlier today with Ms. Young. We have placed an order for 100 gross of ICP-73s at $5,000 per gross for a total price of $500,000. It is my understanding that the transaction will be handled as per the usual agreement. Please notify me immediately if this letter does not conform to your understanding of our agreement.

Your online order form is attached.

Yours truly,

Michael Lubell
VP Purchasing Minicom, Inc.
michael@minicom.nita
Direct phone: (819) 555-2188
www.minicom.nita

MINICOM
PERSONAL CYBER SECURITY

Exhibit 17B

MINICOM
PERSONAL CYBER SECURITY

Minicom, Inc.
724 Science Drive
Nita City, Nita 80027

Phone: (819) 555-2122
Fax: (819) 555-2127
www.minicom.nita

September 23, YR-2

Mr. Chris Kay, Sales Manager
Business Machines Incorporated
1 Industrial Drive
Brookline, MA 02146

Dear Mr. Kay:

This is to confirm my call earlier today with Virginia Young. We have placed an order for 100 gross of ICP-73s at $5,000 per gross for a total price of $500,000. It is my understanding that the transaction will be handled as per the usual agreement. Please notify me immediately if this letter does not conform to your understanding of our agreement.

Yours truly,

Michael Lubell

Michael Lubell
Vice President Purchasing
michael@minicom.nita
Direct phone: (819) 555-2188

ML/jaf
Encl.

Exhibit 17C

BMI Business Machines, Inc.

About BMI ∨ Regional Divisions ∨ News ∨ **Online Ordering ∨** Support ∨

Company: Minicom

Contact Person
First Name: Michael
Last Name: Lubell

Shipping Address: 724 Science Drive

Email: michael@minicom.nita
Phone: (819) 555-2188

City: Nita City
State: NI
Zip Code: 57816

My Order

Item Number	Quantity	Price		
ICP-73	100 Gross	$5,000	Item Total:	**$500,000.00**
			TOTAL:	**$500,000.00**

Add item

BMI will ship your order within 10 or less days utilizing NPS or the carrier of your choosing, with all conditions governed by the U.C.C. Please state any special conditions for this order in the space provided.

Comments/Special Instructions

Confirming call with Ms. Young. Handle shipment per the usual agreement.

Submit

Payment terms: Cash within sixty days. A 2 percent discount (goods only) is given for prompt payment within thirty days; 1.5 percent per month is charged on accounts not paid within sixty days.

We regret that we cannot accept telephone orders. All orders must be in writing using BMI's order form whether by email or mail.

Exhibit 18

Virginia Young

From:	Virginia Young, <virginiayoung.2@bmi.brookline>
Sent:	Fri., 10 Jan YR-1 :12:55 -0500 (EST)
To:	order_confirm@bmi.brookline
Subject:	Work order

Order confirmed today requires shipment immediately of 100 gross of ICP-73 to

Minicom Inc.
724 Science Drive
Nita City, Nita 80027

Ship NPS.
Shipment Date: 1-17-YR-1
Warehouseman: Tim Groody

Exhibit 19A

Michael Lubell

From: Virginia Young <virginiayoung.2@bmi.brookline>
CC: order_confirm@bmi.brookline
Sent: Fri., 10 Jan YR-1 :12:55 -0500 (EST)
To: Michael Lubell <michael@minicom.nita>
Subject: Re: ICP-73 order
Attachment: Minicom_ltr_10JanYR-1.docx; Minicom_stmt_10JanYR-1.docx

Dear Mr. Lubell:

Please see the attached letter and statement from Mr. Kay regarding your order.

Virginia Young
Administrative Assistant to Chris Kay
BMI

From: Michael Lubell <michael@minicom.nita>
Sent: Fri., 10 Jan YR-1 9:37:21 -0700 (MST)
To: Chris Kay <chris.kay@bmi.brookline>
Subject: ICP-73 order

Mr. Kay,

The letter confirming Minicom's phone order is attached. A hard copy is being sent by USPS.

Michael

Michael Lubell
VP Purchasing
Minicom, Inc.
michael@minicom.nita
Direct phone: (819) 555-2188
www.minicom.nita

MINICOM
PERSONAL CYBER SECURITY

Exhibit 19B

BMI

Business Machines, Inc.

One Industrial Drive
Brookline, MA 02146

www.bmi.brookline
(800) BMI-2000
Fax: (800) BMI-2222
Email: info@bmi.brookline

January 10, YR-1

Mr. Michael Lubell
Minicom Incorporated
724 Science Drive
Nita City, NI 80027

Dear Mr. Lubell:

Thank you for your recent order from Business Machines Incorporated. As noted in the attached statement of account, we have shipped your order as per our agreement. Please notify me immediately if the goods are in any way unsatisfactory or if any error appears in your statement.

BMI appreciates your business. Sincerely,

Chris Kay /vey

Chris Kay Sales Manager
Eastern Subdivision II chris.kay@bmi.nita

CK/vy Encl.

Exhibit 19C

BMI

Business Machines, Inc.

One Industrial Drive
Brookline, MA 02146

www.bmi.brookline
(800) BMI-2000
Fax: (800) BMI-2222
Email: info@bmi.brookline

STATEMENT OF ACCOUNT

January 10, YR-1

Minicom Inc.
724 Science Drive
Nita City, NI 80027
Attn: Mr. Michael Lubell

Date	**Items Shipped**	**Debit**	**Credit**
9/6/YR-2		$ 500,000.00	
	Shipping	$ 122.60	
	Insurance	$ 1,110.00	
		$ 501,232.60	
9/25/YR-2	Payment received		$ 491,232.60
	2% credit for prompt payment		$ 10,000.00
BALANCE DUE		**-0-**	
1/10/YR-1	100 Gross ICP- 73	$ 500,000.00	
	Shipping	$ 122.60	
BALANCE DUE		**$ 500,122.60**	

Accounts paid within thirty days receive a 2 percent discount (goods only) for prompt payment. Full payment is due within sixty days. Interest of 1.5 percent per month will be added to accounts after sixty days.

Exhibit 20

NPS
NATIONAL
PARCEL SERVICE

SHIPPING RECORD

SHIPPING RECEIPT—WHITE
NPS COPY—CANARY

RECEIVED FROM

NAME	Business Machines Inc.	DATE	1/17/YR-1
STREET	One Industrial Drive		
CITY/STATE	Brookline, Mass.	ZIP CODE	02146

SEND TO

NAME	MINICOM Inc.		
STREET	724 Science Drive		
CITY/STATE	Nita City, Nita	ZIP CODE	80027

IF COD	DECLARED VALUE	ZONE	
$ ______	$ ______	AIR	GROUND
AMOUNT	AMOUNT		STD

PACKAGE CONTENTS

100 GROSS ICP-73

DO NOT WRITE BELOW THIS LINE

TYPE CHARGE	CUSTOMER COUNTER	DATE	TRAN	CHARGES AMOUNT
COD				
EXCESS				
VALUTATION				
PACKAGE	210			$ 122.65

Unless a greater value is declared in writing on this receipt, the shipper hereby declares and agrees that the released value of each package or article not enclosed in a package covered by this receipt is $100, which is a reasonable value under the circumstances surrounding the transportation. The entry of a DOC amount is not a declaration of value. In addition, the maximum value for an air service shipment is $5,000 and the maximum carrier liability is $5,000. Claims not made to carrier within nine months of shipment date are waived. Customer's check accepted at shipper's risk unless otherwise noted on COD tag.

Exhibit 21

NPS
NATIONAL PARCEL SERVICE

SHIPPING RECORD

SHIPPING RECEIPT—WHITE
NPS COPY—CANARY

RECEIVED FROM

NAME:	Business Machines Inc.	DATE:	1/17/YR-1
STREET:	One Industrial Drive		
CITY/STATE:	Brookline, Mass.	ZIP CODE:	02146

SEND TO

NAME:	MINICOM Inc.		
STREET:	724 Science Drive		
CITY/STATE:	Nita City, Nita	ZIP CODE:	80027

IF COD	DECLARED VALUE	ZONE	
$ ________	$ ________	AIR	GROUND
AMOUNT	AMOUNT		STD

PACKAGE CONTENTS

10 GROSS ICP-73

DO NOT WRITE BELOW THIS LINE

TYPE CHARGE	CUSTOMER COUNTER	DATE	TRAN	CHARGES AMOUNT
COD ________				
EXCESS ________				
VALUTATION ________				
PACKAGE ________	210			$ 30.65

Unless a greater value is declared in writing on this receipt, the shipper hereby declares and agrees that the released value of each package or article not enclosed in a package covered by this receipt is $100, which is a reasonable value under the circumstances surrounding the transportation. The entry of a DOC amount is not a declaration of value. In addition, the maximum value for an air service shipment is $5,000 and the maximum carrier liability is $5,000. Claims not made to carrier within nine months of shipment date are waived. Customer's check accepted at shipper's risk unless otherwise noted on COD tag.

NOTE: Three more of the above receipts appear in the records of BMI and were produced. They are identical in every respect to the one shown above.

Exhibit 22A

NPS
NATIONAL PARCEL SERVICE

SHIPPING RECORD

SHIPPING RECEIPT—WHITE
NPS COPY—CANARY

RECEIVED FROM

NAME:	MINICOM Inc.	DATE:	1/24/YR-1
STREET:	724 Science Drive		
CITY/STATE:	Nita City, Nita	ZIP CODE:	80027

SEND TO

NAME:	Business Machines Inc.		
STREET:	One Industrial Drive		
CITY/STATE:	Brookline, Mass.	ZIP CODE:	02146

IF COD	DECLARED VALUE	ZONE	
		AIR	GROUND
$ ________ AMOUNT	$ ________ AMOUNT		STD

PACKAGE CONTENTS

10 GROSS ICP-22

DO NOT WRITE BELOW THIS LINE

TYPE CHARGE	CUSTOMER COUNTER	DATE	TRAN	CHARGES AMOUNT
COD	$115,000		Insurance:	$ 270.50
			Shipping	30.25
EXCESS VALUTATION				$ 300.15
PACKAGE	210			

Unless a greater value is declared in writing on this receipt, the shipper hereby declares and agrees that the released value of each package or article not enclosed in a package covered by this receipt is $100, which is a reasonable value under the circumstances surrounding the transportation. The entry of a DOC amount is not a declaration of value. In addition, the maximum value for an air service shipment is $5,000 and the maximum carrier liability is $5,000. Claims not made to carrier within nine months of shipment date are waived. Customer's check accepted at shipper's risk unless otherwise noted on COD tag.

Thank you for using NATIONAL PARCEL SERVICE

NOTE: Three more of the above receipts appear in the records of BMI and were produced. They are identical in every respect to the one shown above.

Exhibit 22B

MINICOM
PERSONAL CYBER SECURITY

Minicom, Inc.
724 Science Drive
Nita City, Nita 80027

Phone: (819) 555-2122
Fax: (819) 555-2127
www.minicom.nita

January 24, YR-1

Mr. Chris Kay
Business Machines Incorporated 1 Industrial Drive
Brookline, MA 02146

Dear Mr. Kay:

We received today a shipment of 40 gross of ICP-22s from your Eastern Warehouse No. 22 mislabeled as ICP-73. As your records should reflect, our order was for <u>100</u> gross of ICP-73s. We have today returned the incorrect shipment. Shipping and insurance for the return comes to $300.75. Please remit this amount at your earliest convenience.

In reviewing your bill of 1/10/YR-1, I have noted that you failed to charge us for insurance on your last shipment. Please make the necessary correction.

Our Vice President for Production informs me that we will need the parts by January 31, YR-1, for a large April 1 order. Please advise me immediately as to when we can expect delivery.

Thank you for your prompt attention to this matter.

Yours truly,

Michael Lubell

Michael Lubell
Vice President Purchasing
michael@minicom.nita
Direct phone: (819) 555-2188

ML/jaf

Exhibit 23

Michael Lubell

From: Chris Kay, <chris.kay@bmi.brookline>
Sent: Mon, 27 Jan YR-1 09:42:36 -0500 (EDT)
To: Michael Lubell <michael@minicom.nita>
Subject: Returned merchandise

Dear Mr. Lubell:

Thank you for the return of the goods erroneously sent to you by Business Machines Incorporated. Your account will be credited for the full amount of shipping and insurance charges for the return. As we have risk-of-loss insurance, in the unlikely event this situation occurs again, there is no need for you to insure any shipment of goods to BMI.

Our records indicate that the shipment of 100 gross of ICP-73s was sent via NPS prepaid on 1/17/YR-1. We have contacted NPS, and they are tracing the shipment. We apologize for any delay caused by their error.

I expect you will receive your order in the very near future. BMI appreciates your business.

Sincerely,

Chris Kay Sales Manager
Eastern Subdivision II
chris.kay@bmi.brookline

Exhibit 24

Text from Elliot Milstein to Michael Lubell

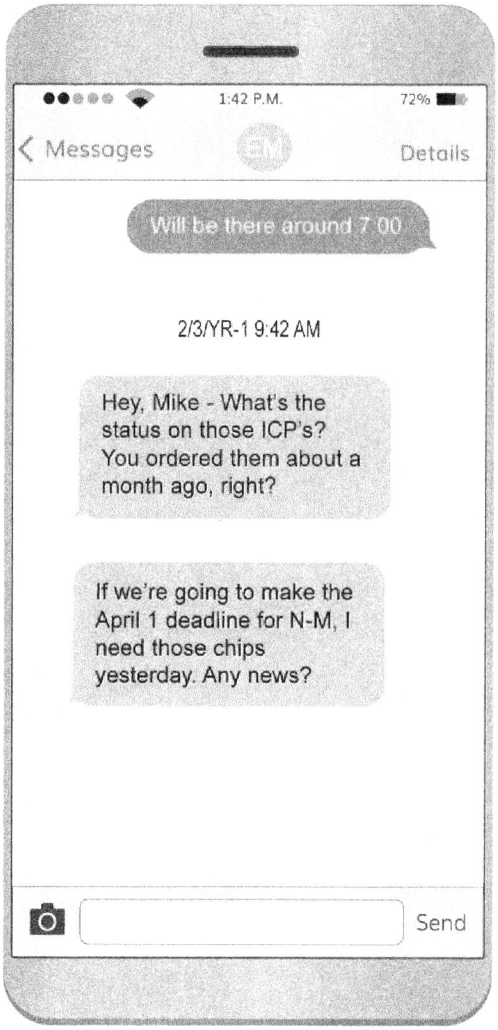

Exhibit 25

Text from Michael Lubell to Elliot Milstein

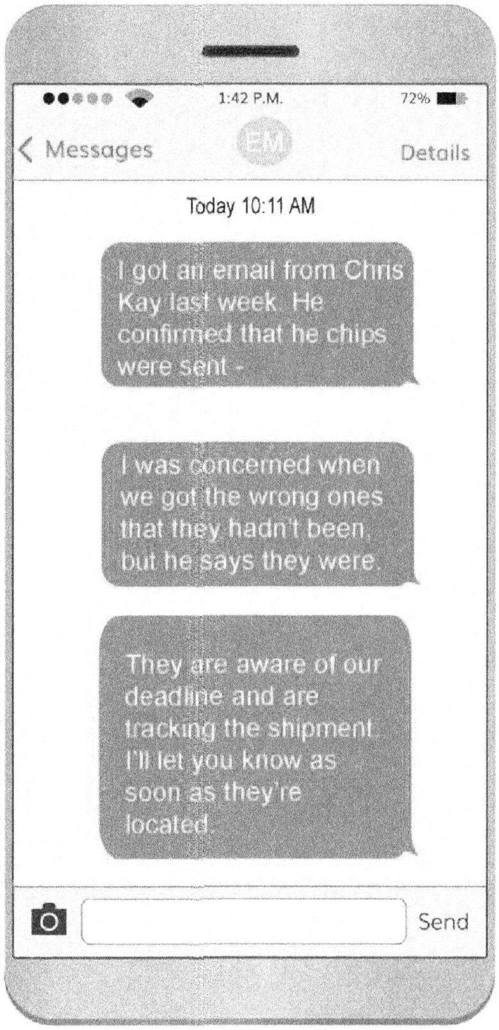

Exhibit 26A

BMI

Business Machines, Inc.

One Industrial Drive
Brookline, MA 02146

www.bmi.brookline
(800) BMI-2000
Fax: (800) BMI-2222
Email: info@bmi.brookline

February 14, YR-1

Mr. Michael Lubell
Minicom Inc.
24 Science Drive
Nita City, NI 80027

Dear Mr. Lubell:

I have finally heard from NPS regarding your missing shipment. After much prodding, they finally admitted that the shipment was lost by them. Their check for $400.00, the full amount of their admitted liability, is enclosed. As you will note, I have endorsed it over to you. Should you wish to discuss this matter with NPS, their Claims Manager is Sharon Cupitt.

We have replenished our supply of ICP-73s and stand ready to fill any future orders at our current prices. However, as I informed Elliot at Hilton Head, our prices will go up 10 percent on March 1.

BMI appreciates your business.

Sincerely,

Chris Kay

Chris Kay
Sales Manager
Eastern Subdivision II
chris.kay@bmi.brookline

Exhibit 26B

NPS
NATIONAL
PARCEL SERVICE

0225

February 11,YR-1

PAY TO THE ORDER OF:

Business Machines Inc. $ 400.00

Four hundred and no/100 DOLLARS

NATIONAL PARCEL SERVICE

THE CITIZENS & SOUTHERN
NATIONAL BANK
SAVANNAH, GEORGIA

Pay to the order of
Mini-Com
John L. Ross
Asst. Cntlr.

Exhibit 27A

MINICOM

PERSONAL CYBER SECURITY

Employee: Michael Lubell

Call Log | Voicemail | Fax | Settings

Person Called | Number | Business Purpose

Date	Person Called/ **Calling**	Number	Business Purpose
2/21/YR-1	NPS Sharon Cupitt	428-3134	NPS liability w/o insurance is $100 per package.
2/21/YR-1	BMI Chris Kay	800-264-2000	Called re: lost order. Kay says it's our problem. Says we didn't request insurance.
2/21/YR-1	Kalo's Katering	887-5397	Changed sandwiches from pastrami to turkey for exec. lunch.
2/21/YR-1	Opp's Plumbing	347-2281	Told them that bill will not be paid until toilet is properly fixed.
2/21/YR-1	**Brown's Body Shop**		Wife's car will cost $825 for repairs.
2/21/YR-1	Potter's Pharmacy	273-4189	Ordered refill on Lexapro. Generic now available. Will be ready at 5 p.m.

Exhibit 27B

Lubell, Michael
Escitalopram Oxalate 10 Mg Tag Acco
NDC: 16729-0169001

Generic For > Lexapro 10 Mg Tab Alle

TAKE ONE TABLET BY MOUTH EVERY DAY

2.00 Refills of 90 until 07/01/YR+1

Drg Exp. 12/12/YR+2 BLANAK, MICAH (819) 555-3856

RX# 839682 FIRST FILL DATE: 01/05/YR-1

TAFT-HANSON PHARMACY
39245 MAPLE BLVD
NITA CITY, NITA 57813

(819) 555-2874

This medicine is a white, round-shaped, scored, film-coated tablet imprinted with 10 (Biconvex White to off-white)

May Make You Drowsy Or Dizzy. Do Not Drink Alcohol With This Drug. Use Care When Operating A Vehicle, Vessel, Or Other Machines.

If You Are Pregnant, Plan To Become Pregnant, Or Are Breast-Feeding, Talk With Your Doctor.

Do Not Take Other Medicines Without Checking With Your Doctor Or Pharmacist.

Exhibit 28

Michael Lubell

From: Michael Lubell <michael@minicom.nita>
Sent: Fri., 21 Feb YR-1 14:13:09 -0700 (MST)
To: Elliot Milstein <elliot@minicom.nita>
Subject: BMI shipment

As I mentioned several days ago, we are having trouble with our shipment of ICP-73s from BMI. I called Chris Kay, and he says they will not assume any liability. He says that in the absence of a specific request they do not insure and he received no word from his administrative assistant that I requested insurance. He also says that my confirming letter, which clearly states the transaction was to be on the same terms as the last when they did insure, was not understood that way by him. My phone log, by the way, does indicate his assistant was told to get insurance on the shipment for its full value and agreed to the same.

I know you have a personal relationship with Kay, and I suggest you contact him directly. I do not believe I can accomplish anything further on this matter. NPS, of course, takes the position that their liability in the absence of insurance is limited to $400. We have a check for that amount, which we have not deposited.

Michael Lubell
Vice President Purchasing
michael@minicom.nita
Direct phone: (819) 555-2188

MINICOM
PERSONAL CYBER SECURITY

Exhibit 29

MINICOM

PERSONAL CYBER SECURITY

Employee: Elliot Milstein

Call Log | Voicemail | Fax | Settings

Person Called | Number | Business Purpose

Date	Person Called/ **Calling**	Number	Business Purpose
2/21/YR-1	Chris Kay	800-264-2000	Will check out problem with legal dept. and write ASAP.
2/21/YR-1	Horton, Stein & Benson	343-2180	Made appt. for 2/25 at Kalo's Kitchen for lunch meeting.

Exhibit 30

BMI

Business Machines, Inc.

One Industrial Drive
Brookline, MA 02146

www.bmi.brookline
(800) BMI-2000
Fax: (800) BMI-2222
Email: info@bmi.brookline

March 3, YR-1

Mr. Elliot Milstein
Minicom Inc.
724 Science Drive
Nita City, NI 80027

Dear Mr. Milstein:

I have reviewed with our legal department the status of our recent transaction. Under the terms of our contract, as controlled by the Uniform Commercial Code, the risk of loss of this shipment clearly falls upon your company. We regret to inform you that we cannot be responsible for the losses your company has incurred and must instead demand that you make payment of the amounts due BMI as shown in our previous billing to you.

I am informed that all subsequent correspondence about this matter should be referred to Mr. John W. Davis in our General Counsel's office.

Sincerely,

Chris Kay

Chris Kay
Sales Manager
Eastern Subdivision II
chris.kay@bmi.brookline

CK/vy
Encl.
cc: John W. Davis

Exhibit 31

MINICOM
PERSONAL CYBER SECURITY

Minicom, Inc.
724 Science Drive
Nita City, Nita 80027

Phone: (819) 555-2122
Fax: (819) 555-2127
www.minicom.nita

March 7, YR-1

Mr. Chris Kay
Business Machines Incorporated
One Industrial Drive
Brookline, MA 02146

Dear Mr. Kay:

When we met in Hilton Head last December, you assured me that in dealing with Business Machines Incorporated I would find your company to be concerned with the success of my business. As you know, we are a young company and cannot afford substantial losses that are avoidable, so we take every precaution necessary to safeguard our working capital. When we ordered the ICP-73s from your company in September, we requested that you send them insured and you did. We made the same request at the time of the January order. This time BMI did not comply, and your failure, you claim, should cost us $500,000 plus the $50,000 price increase that has gone into effect since our first order.

If anyone deserves to bear this cost, it is BMI. Our company did everything possible to avoid the loss; BMI failed to do anything to help us in this regard. Contrary to the language of your company's slogan, "BMI appreciates your business," it looks to me that the correct statement is "BMI gives you the business."

I have referred this matter to our attorney, and you will be hearing from him in the future.

Sincerely,

Elliot Milstein

Elliot Milstein President
elliot@minicom.biz

EM/jaf
cc: Charles A. Horton

Exhibit 32

MINICOM

PERSONAL CYBER SECURITY

Employee: Michael Lubell

Call Log | Voicemail | Fax | Settings

Person Called | Number | Business Purpose

Date	Person Called/ Calling	Number	Business Purpose
3/10/YR-1	Gold's Delicatessen	381-4262	Ordered exec. lunch.
3/10/YR-1	Exrox Inc. Brent Taylor	617-429-3800	Ordered 100g MICP-2 (same as ICP-73). Ship NPS. 550K.
3/10/YR-1	Computer Innovations Les Ottolenghi	387-2188	Asked about sales openings. Sent resume.
3/10/YR-1	Dell Corp.	394-5087	Ditto

Exhibit 33

Michael Lubell

From:	Michael Lubell <michael@minicom.nita>
Sent:	Mon, 10 Mar YR-1 11:07:10 -0700 (MST)
To:	btaylor@exrox.nita
Subject:	Order

Mr. Taylor,

This is to confirm our phone conversation earlier today, in which we agreed to the following transaction. Exrox agrees to sell 100 gross of interlaced graphene computing platforms (your part number MICP-2) at $5,500.00 per gross for a total price of $550,000. Minicom may pay the full price within 30 days of receipt and receive a 2% discount for prompt payment. Payment after 30 days, but before 60 days, will be at full price. Payment after 60 days will include 1% per month finance charge. Exrox agrees to ship via NPS. Minicom agrees to pay all shipping costs.

Please notify me immediately if the above does not adequately reflect our agreement.

Michael

Michael Lubell
VP Purchasing
Minicom, Inc.
www.minicom.nita

MINICOM
PERSONAL CYBER SECURITY

Exhibit 34A

Michael Lubell

From:	Brent Taylor, <bataylor @exrox.brookline>
Sent:	Fri, 14 Mar YR-1 14:37:10 -0500 (EDT)
To:	Michael Lubell <michael@minicom.nita>
Subject:	ICP Order
Attachments:	Statement.docx

Dear Mr. Lubell:

Thank you for your recent order, which has been shipped today. Please let me know if the merchandise is satisfactory.

Your statement is enclosed. Sincerely,

Brent A. Taylor
Sales Manager
Microcomputer Parts

Exhibit 34B

EXROX®

One Computer Drive
Brookline, Massachusetts 02146

Tel.: (617) 429-3800
Fax: (617) 429-2900

March 14, YR-1

STATEMENT OF ACCOUNT

Minicom Inc.
724 Science Drive
Nita City, Nita 80027

Date	Goods Shipped	Price	Payment	Balance
3/14/YR-1	100 gross MICP-2	$ 550,00.00		
	Ship via NPS	140.60		$ 550,140.60

Interest will be charged on accounts after sixty days at the rate of 1 percent/month or part thereof.

Exhibit 35

Elliot Milstein

From:	Elliot Milstein <elliot@minicom.nita>
Sent:	27 Mar YR-1 09:30:10 -0700 (MST)
To:	gsmith@neimanmarcus.nita
Subject:	CyberShield Order

Greg:

We have encountered a supplier problem and will not be able to make the April 1 deadline for the CyberShields—can you give me a couple extra weeks? The product will be first-rate.

Exhibit 36

Elliot Milstein

From:	gsmith@neimanmarcus.nita
Sent:	27 Mar YR-1 16:30:10 -0700 (MST)
To:	Elliot Milstein <elliot@minicom.nita>
Subject:	RE: CyberShield Order

Elliot

I am so sorry I cannot accommodate you. Had to call other bidder on contract. They can provide immediately—my superiors insist on going with the sure thing. Hope we can do some business in the future, but we are out for now.

Sorry again.

Greg

Exhibit 37

EXROX®

One Computer Drive
Brookline, Massachusetts 02146

Tel.: (617) 429-3800
Fax: (617) 429-2900

June 13, YR-1

STATEMENT OF ACCOUNT

Minicom Inc.
724 Science Drive
Nita City, NI 80027

Date	Goods Shipped	Price	Payment	Balance
3/14/YR-1	100 gross MICP-2	$ 550,00.00		
	Ship via NPS	140.60		$ 550,140.60
6/13/YR-1	Interest	$5,500.00		**$ 555,640.60**
			Balance Now Due	**$ 555,640.60**

Interest will be charged on accounts after sixty days at the rate of 1 percent/month or part thereof.

Exhibit 38A

MINICOM
PERSONAL CYBER SECURITY

Minicom, Inc.
724 Science Drive
Nita City, Nita 80027

Phone: (819) 555-2122
Fax: (819) 555-2127
www.minicom.nita

June 20, YR-1

Mr. Brent Taylor
EXROX Incorporated 1 Computer Drive
Brookline, MA 02146

Dear Mr. Taylor:

Thank you for your recent delivery of MICP-2 interlaced graphene computing platforms. We apologize for our delay in payment, which was a result of differences with a former supplier. Our check for the purchase price plus interest is enclosed.

We look forward to doing business with you in the future.

Yours truly,

Michael Lubell

Michael Lubell
Vice President Purchasing
michael@minicom.nita

ML/jaf
Encl.

Exhibit 38B

MINICOM INC.	2115
724 Science Drive Nita City, Nita 80027 Phone (720) 555-1212	June 20 YR-1
PAY TO THE ORDER OF:	
Exrox Incorporated	$ 555,640.60
Five hundred fifty-five thousand six hundred forty and 60/100	DOLLARS
Nita National Bank Nita City, Nita 80027	Elliot Milstein
*Memo*______________________________	

ENDORSE CHECK HERE:

X

PAY TO THE ORDER OF
Exrox Incorporated
NITA NATIONAL BANK
Nita City, Nita 80027
FOR DEPOSIT ONLY

General Jury Instructions

NITA Instruction 01:01—Introduction

You have been selected as jurors and have taken an oath to well and truly try this cause. This trial will last one day.

During the progress of the trial there will be periods of time when the Court recesses. During those periods of time, you must not talk about this case among yourselves or with anyone else.

During the trial, do not talk to any of the parties, their lawyers, or any of the witnesses.

If any attempt is made by anyone to talk to you concerning the matters here under consideration, you should immediately report that fact to the Court.

You should keep an open mind. You should not form or express an opinion during the trial and should reach no conclusion in this case until you have heard all of the evidence, the arguments of counsel, and the final instructions as to the law that will be given to you by the Court.

NITA Instruction 01:02—Conduct of the Trial

First, the attorneys will have an opportunity to make opening statements. These statements are not evidence and should be considered only as a preview of what the attorneys expect the evidence will be.

Following the opening statements, witnesses will be called to testify. They will be placed under oath and questioned by the attorneys. Documents and other tangible exhibits may also be received as evidence. If an exhibit is given to you to examine, you should examine it carefully, individually, and without any comment.

It is counsel's right and duty to object when testimony or other evidence is being offered that he or she believes is not admissible.

When the Court sustains an objection to a question, the jurors must disregard the question and the answer, if one has been given, and draw no inference from the question or answer or speculate as to what the witness would have said if permitted to answer. Jurors must also disregard evidence stricken from the record.

When the Court sustains an objection to any evidence the jurors must disregard that evidence.

When the Court overrules an objection to any evidence, the jurors must not give that evidence any more weight than if the objection had not been made.

When the evidence is completed, the attorneys will make closing arguments. These arguments are not evidence but are given to help you evaluate the evidence. The attorneys are also permitted to argue in an attempt to persuade you to a particular verdict. You may accept or reject those arguments as you see fit.

Finally, just before you retire to consider your verdict, I will give you further instructions on the law that applies to this case.

NITA INSTRUCTION 2:01—INTRODUCTION

Members of the jury, the evidence and arguments in this case have been completed, and I will now instruct you as to the law.

The law applicable to this case is stated in these instructions, and it is your duty to follow all of them.

You must not single out certain instructions and disregard others.

It is your duty to determine the facts and to determine them only from the evidence in this case. You are to apply the law to the facts and in this way decide the case. You must not be governed or influenced by sympathy or prejudice for or against any party in this case. Your verdict must be based on evidence and not on speculation, guess, or conjecture.

The evidence that you should consider consists only of witness testimony and exhibits the Court has received.

Any evidence that was received for a limited purpose should not be considered by you for any other purpose.

You should consider all the evidence in the light of your own observations and experiences in life.

NITA INSTRUCTION 2:02—OPENING STATEMENTS AND CLOSING ARGUMENTS

Opening statements are made by the attorneys to acquaint you with the facts they expect to prove. Closing arguments are made by the attorneys to discuss the facts and circumstances in the case and should be confined to the evidence and to reasonable inferences to be drawn therefrom. Neither opening statements nor closing arguments are evidence, and any statement or argument made by the attorneys that is not based on the evidence should be disregarded.

NITA INSTRUCTION 2:03—CREDIBILITY OF WITNESSES

You are the sole judges of the credibility of the witnesses and of the weight to be given to the testimony of each witness. In determining what credit is to be given any witness, you may take into account his ability and opportunity to observe; his manner and appearance while testifying; any interest, bias, or prejudice he may have; the reasonableness of his testimony considered in the light of all the evidence; and any other factors that bear on the believability and weight of the witness's testimony.

NITA INSTRUCTION 2:04—BURDEN OF PROOF

When I say that a party has the burden of proof on any issue or use the expression "if you find," "if you decide," or "by a preponderance of the evidence," I mean that you must be persuaded from a consideration of all the evidence in the case that the issue in question is more probably true than not true.

Any findings of fact you make must be based on probabilities, not possibilities. It may not be based on surmise, speculation, or conjecture.

Proposed Jury Instructions Specific to This Case

1. Introduction

The Court now will instruct you as to the claims and defenses of each party and the law governing the case. You must arrive at your verdict by applying the law, as I now instruct you, to the facts as you find them to be.

2. Background—Basic Contentions of the Parties

The parties to this case are Business Machines Incorporated, the plaintiff, and Minicom Incorporated, the defendant. BMI has sued Minicom, seeking to recover damages based on a claim that Minicom failed to pay for certain goods as required by a contract. Both sides agree that the goods were lost in transit. Minicom contends that the contract required BMI to take out insurance to protect against the loss, but that BMI failed to do so. BMI denies that the contract required it to take out insurance.

3. Damages—General

If BMI prevails, its damages will be predicated on the price of the goods that it shipped to Minicom. If Minicom prevails, its damages will be set according to the difference between the price of the goods ordered from BMI and the price of the more expensive goods it ordered from another supplier, Exrox, when the BMI parts did not arrive. Minicom also claims damages for a contract with Nieman Marcus that it allegedly lost because it had not received the BMI parts. BMI denies Minicom's claims for damages, and Minicom denies BMI's claim. I will return to this issue of damages in more detail later.

4. Existence of a Contract

You first must decide whether BMI has proven that there was a contract for the sale of the parts to Minicom. BMI has the burden of proving this issue by the preponderance of the evidence. BMI must prove all elements of the contract about which the parties do not agree. BMI must prove that there was an offer, an acceptance, and mutual assent. BMI must also prove that the goods were delivered to National Parcel Service. You must consider all facts and circumstances in deciding whether BMI made the delivery.

An offer is an expression of one's willingness to be bound by a contract. An acceptance is an expression of assent to the offer. Mutual assent occurs when an offer is communicated by one party to another and is accepted by the other party.

Whether there was mutual assent must be determined from the conduct of the parties. Whether that conduct constituted an offer and acceptance and, if it did, what its meaning was depends on what reasonable persons in the positions of the parties would have thought they meant. In determining what reasonable persons would have thought the conduct meant, you should consider the evidence as to all circumstances existing at the time of the offer or acceptance. You should not consider any different, but unexpressed meanings intended by either party.

5. Was Insurance by BMI a Term of the Contract?

If you decide that BMI proved that there was a contract between the parties for the purchase of goods from BMI by Minicom, you next must decide whether that contract included a term requiring BMI to insure the goods. Minicom has the burden of proving that term by the greater weight of the evidence. The term of insurance may be proved by showing: 1) that there was an oral contract providing for insurance; or 2) that there was a written contract for insurance. If after applying this standard you find that BMI proved a contract and Minicom did not prove a term of insurance, you will next consider BMI's damages. If you find that BMI proved a contract and Minicom proved a term of insurance, you will move on to consider Minicom's damages. [If you find that neither party proved a contract, the case is ended, and you will return to the courtroom to deliver your verdict.]

6. Agency

In order for Minicom to prove an oral contract between Minicom and BMI providing for a term of insurance, Minicom must prove by the greater weight of the evidence that Virginia Young was acting as an agent of BMI on January 6, YR-1, in her telephone conversation with Michael Lubell and that she had the authority to contract for BMI. Agency is the relationship that results when one person or company, called the principal, authorizes another person, called the agent, to act for that principal. This relationship may be created by word of mouth, or by writing, or it may be implied from conduct amounting to consent or acquiescence.

A principal is liable to others for the acts of the agent in the transaction of the principal's business. In this case, to make BMI liable under the doctrine of agency for the acts of Virginia Young, Minicom must prove three things by the greater weight of the evidence:

(a) That there was a principal-agent relationship between BMI and Virginia Young on January 6, YR-1;

(b) That Virginia Young was engaged in the business of BMI at that time;

(c) That the business in which Virginia Young was engaged was within the course and scope of her employment and authority. It would be within the course and scope of her employment and authority if it was done in furtherance of the business of BMI, or if it was incidental to the duties entrusted to Virginia Young by BMI, or if it was done in carrying out a direction or an order of BMI.

7. Damages

A party injured by a breach of contract is entitled to be placed in the same position it would have occupied if the contract had been performed, insofar as this can be done by the awarding of money damages. To recover damages, the burden of proof is on the party damaged by the breach to prove by the greater weight of the evidence, first, that it sustained damages in some amount and, second, the amount of those damages.

8. BMI's Damages

If you find that there was a contract with no term of insurance, you must award BMI the price of the goods, plus shipping and interest, as required by the contract, since Minicom has agreed that the contract called for payment of that amount and no payment has been made. If, however, you find that contract had a term requiring BMI to insure, Minicom is the party injured by the breach, and BMI recovers nothing.

9. Minicom's Damages

If you find that it was a term of the contract that BMI would insure the goods, you must decide if Minicom was injured by BMI's breach in failing to insure, i.e., whether Minicom made a reasonable purchase of goods from Exrox in substitution for those due from BMI and that Minicom did so in good faith and without unreasonable delay. If you find that Minicom did this, Minicom is entitled to recover the difference between the cost of the substituted goods from Exrox and its cost under the original contract with BMI.

Minicom also makes a further claim for consequential loss—that it lost a contract with Nieman Marcus because of BMI's breach of contract. You must decide whether Minicom has proven, by the greater weight of the evidence, a) that it had a contract with Neiman Marcus, b) that it lost profits on that contract because of BMI's failure to insure the shipment, and c) the amount of the profits, if any, that Minicom lost on such contract.